Negative Hallucinosis in Wilfred Bion's Theory of Transformations

In this illuminating volume, Rodrigo Barahona takes up the question of transformations in hallucinosis in Wilfred Bion's work.

The book discusses how the analyst's functioning, his receptivity and ability to make sense out of what is unconsciously occurring between himself and the patient, and the ability to find words to represent it—the basic psychoanalytic task—is enhanced when the distinction between two basic types of transformations in hallucinosis can be borne in mind: transformations in positive hallucinosis and transformations in negative hallucinosis. In the psychoanalytic literature, this distinction has not been formally established, with the general term "transformations in hallucinosis" used for both processes. This book cuts a clearer distinction between the two, describing their distinct though overlapping metapsychologies, and charts the clinical implications. In making these distinctions, the book draws on André Green's work, arguing for a continuity between Green's negative hallucination and Bion's theory of thinking and transformations in negative hallucinosis. The clinical implications of working with this concept are discussed in relation to the work of contemporary psychoanalytic authors such as Civitarese, Cassorla, Mawson, and Meltzer.

By drawing comparisons and making specific connections between the work of Bion and Green, and extending these connections to the clinical and metapsychological writings of leading contemporary analysts, *Negative Hallucinosis in Wilfred Bion's Theory of Transformations* will be of great interest to practitioners and scholars at all levels interested in the work of Wilfred Bion and this extension to his theory of transformations.

Rodrigo Barahona is a psychoanalyst and faculty member at the Boston Psychoanalytic Society & Institute and the Massachusetts Institute for Psychoanalysis. He is on the board of directors of the *Boston Group for Psychoanalytic Studies* and of the *Psychoanalytic Quarterly*. He is a member of the American Psychoanalytic Association and the International Psychoanalytic Association and has a private psychoanalytic practice in Brookline, Massachusetts.

The Routledge Wilfred R. Bion Studies Book Series
Series Editor
Howard B. Levine, MD

The contributions of Wilfred Bion are among the most cited in the analytic literature. Their appeal lies not only in their content and explanatory value, but in their generative potential. Although Bion's training and many of his clinical instincts were deeply rooted in the classical tradition of Melanie Klein, his ideas have a potentially universal appeal. Rather than emphasizing a particular psychic content (e.g., Oedipal conflicts in need of resolution; splits that needed to be healed; preconceived transferences that must be allowed to form and flourish, etc.), he tried to help open and prepare the mind of the analyst (without memory, desire or theoretical preconception) for the encounter with the patient.

Bion's formulations of group mentality and the psychotic and non-psychotic portions of the mind, his theory of thinking and emphasis on facing and articulating the truth of one's existence so that one might truly learn first hand from one's own experience, his description of psychic development (alpha-function and container/contained) and his exploration of **O** are "non-denominational" concepts that defy relegation to a particular school or orientation of psychoanalysis. Consequently, his ideas have taken root in many places . . . and those ideas continue to inform many different branches of psychoanalytic inquiry and interest.[1]

It is with this heritage and its promise for the future developments of psychoanalysis in mind that we present *The Routledge Wilfred Bion Studies Book Series*. This series gathers together under newly emerging and continually evolving contributions to psychoanalytic thinking that rest upon Bion's foundational texts and explore and extend the implications of his thought. For a full list of titles in the series, please visit the Routledge website at: https://www.routledge.com/The-Routledge-Wilfred-Bion-Studies-Book-Series/book-series/RWBSBS

Note

1 Levine, H. B. & Civitarese, G. (2016) Editors' Preface. In *The W.R. Bion Tradition*, edited by H. B. Levine & G. Civitarese. London: Karnac, 2016, p. xxi.

Negative Hallucinosis in Wilfred Bion's Theory of Transformations

On Finding One's Ghost

Rodrigo Barahona

Routledge
Taylor & Francis Group

LONDON AND NEW YORK

Designed cover image: © Getty

First published 2025
by Routledge
4 Park Square, Milton Park, Abingdon, Oxon OX14 4RN

and by Routledge
605 Third Avenue, New York, NY 10158

Routledge is an imprint of the Taylor & Francis Group, an informa business

© 2025 Rodrigo Barahona

British Library Cataloguing-in-Publication Data
A catalogue record for this book is available from the British Library

ISBN: 978-1-032-85975-0 (hbk)
ISBN: 978-1-032-79792-2 (pbk)
ISBN: 978-1-003-52074-0 (ebk)

DOI: 10.4324/9781003520740

Typeset in Times New Roman
by Apex CoVantage, LLC

For Brigitte, Ophelia, and Gael

Contents

Acknowledgments

As is usually the case in a community as vivacious, passionate, and committed to their work as that of psychoanalysts, there are many people to whom I am grateful for inspiring me to think and do the clinical work that led me down the long road to this book. At the start of my career: Phyllis Meadow, Chris Healy, Jane Snyder, Stephen Soldz, and Mara Wagner of the Boston Graduate School of Psychoanalysis. My work at BGSP, a graduate school like no other, and with these analysts in particular, taught me the value of immersion in group process and deep listening to countertransference, aggression, narcissism, and regressed states. They also offered me my first experiences with academic writing and had enough faith in my abilities to ask me to teach when I was still only a young graduate. It was in a seminar with Phyllis Meadow in 2004, on *The Work of the Negative* by André Green that I first became familiar with his work, the core of which is at the center of this book in relation to Bion's ideas. Lew Kirshner, who supervised some of my earlier hospital out-patient work and encouraged me to apply to full psychoanalytic training; the faculty and fellow candidates at the Psychoanalytic Institute of New England (PINE), where I completed my full psychoanalytic training, in particular Susan Rosbrow-Reich, Jane Kite, Sarah Ackerman, Fred Busch, Evelyn Schwaber, Jim Barron, and Axel Hoffer. At PINE, I was also encouraged to teach and write and received careful attention to the quality of my work by very attentive analysts who conveyed a deep appreciation for the craft of analysis. My colleagues and students at the Boston Psychoanalytic Society and Institute (BPSI) and the Massachusetts Institute for Psychoanalysis (MIP) who have stimulated my involvement with psychoanalytic institutions and learning; my friends and fellow board members from the Boston Group for Psychoanalytic Studies (BGPS), Jack Foehl, Christopher Lovett, David Power, Dolan Power, Karen Roos, and in particular Larry Brown and Howard Levine, whose support for my work and this book has been invaluable. I am deeply grateful for their friendship and guidance over the past decade and for their setting a high bar by example for Bionian scholarship, encouraging my connections with international psychoanalysis and deepening my understanding of the work of Bion. My colleagues on the editorial boards of the *Psychoanalytic Quarterly*, the *International Journal of Psychoanalysis*, and the *Journal of the American Psychoanalytic Association*. Of these I am particularly grateful to Lucy Lafarge, Richard Zimmer, Daria Colombo, Jay Greenberg, and Mitch Wilson, who have supported and encouraged my writing and my involvement in the greater psychoanalytic community. At *JAPA*, Gabriela Legorreta and Mina Levinsky-Wohl deserve my deepest gratitude for having faith in my writing early on and encouraging me to contribute to the foreign book review section. I owe a special debt to my close friend, mentor, colleague, and family member, Eddy Carrillo, whose continued invitations for me to teach candidates at the *Association for Social-Critical Psychoanalysis* in San José, Costa Rica, have helped me stay in touch with the psychoanalysis of my country of birth, as well as given me opportunities to develop my thinking. Eddy too bolstered my faith in myself as someone who could think and do this work, first as my teacher in my undergraduate psychology program and throughout the years in our close connection that has developed since. For my sister, Kathia Barahona, who already a psychology student, noticed her younger brother at a crossroads in life and had the good sense to know he might be interested in what she was reading at the time, which turned out to be Lacan. Since then, I never turned back from this beautiful profession. For my mother and father for tolerating those years of uncertainty about what I would do with my life and believing in me when I made my choice; to Alistair McKnight, for our close friendship, rooted in our common experiences of relocation, growing professionally, having families, and being-becoming psychoanalysts; to my wife, Brigitte Zakari, for our never-ending conversations about the profession we share and love, and whose support in the family we created and the life we live makes it possible for me to write; My patients, past and present, who trust me with their stories and inner lives and who share with me so much of their time.

To everyone mentioned in these acknowledgments, I owe this book.

April 1, 2024
Watertown, Massachusetts

Introduction

What did Bion mean by *transformations in hallucinosis*? How is this term used differently in our psychoanalytic literature? What are the clinical implications and problems related to confusions around the term? Are there such things as transformations in *negative hallucinosis*, and if so, what differentiates them from transformations in *positive hallucinosis*? What are the clinical implications of this differentiation? How do transformations in negative hallucinosis relate to other established concepts in our field, such as André Green's *the work of the negative*, *the dead mother*, and *the negative hallucination of thought and thinking*; Roosevelt Cassorla's *enactment and non-dreaming*; and Meltzer's *claustrum*? How do transformations in negative hallucinosis relate to the man Bion himself and his traumatic personal history in the first World War? These are the questions I set out to explore in this book.

It was once said of Wilfred Bion that he had the ability to "sit(ting) farther from his own face than any other man I know".[1] It is perhaps from this vantage point that Bion was able to survey and map out for us the principles, the horizontal and vertical positions, the terrain and ground features that make up the cartography of the formless infinite constituting the psychotic and non-psychotic parts of the mind. Among these features are concepts that, within his model, relate to each other in constant conjunction, ever expanding and deepening the edges and depths of our understanding. Many of Bion's ideas are well-known even among analysts from differing schools of thought, for example: alpha-function, alpha and beta-elements, container-contained, learning from experience, dreaming the session, transformations, negative capability, and reverie. Most analysts today attribute to Bion, rightly or wrongly, the intersubjectivation of Klein's concept of projective identification, a step that has proven over time to be of immense clinical value in substantiating Klein's model for the projection and embodiment of internal objects in self and other, as well as for thinking about the permeability between unconscious phantasy and the construction of the perception of external reality. Bion's extension of Klein's idea has also had important implications for how objects in external reality *feel* about themselves as well as *act* in relation to the projector. For instance, Bion's (1962a) elaborations on what he called normal or realistic projective identification provided analysts with a way of thinking about what they disturbingly, or at least

DOI: 10.4324/9781003520740-1

uncomfortably, experienced as intrusive countertransference without any other way of formulating for themselves what they otherwise regarded as private resistance or the patient's induced aggression. Nevertheless, Bion's theoretical armament, perhaps because of its wide-ranging clinical reach, can sometimes suffer from the lack of precision that comes with extensive use.[2]

Yet another reason for the fuzziness around some of Bion's notions may be the easy conflation of meaning between them, given that in Bion's style of theory construction, concepts tend to derive dialectically from each other or are interconnected through mutual valence, such as container-contained, negative capability and Faith, and group basic assumptions and O. The meaning of the concepts employed in Bion's language, and as will be experienced in reading this book, is co-constructed between their inherent content and their relationship to each other. Bion's system is ever constantly-conjoining, ever expanding, and within these transformations the theoretical specificity of the type that grounds good, clinical interventions may sometimes get lost. When this happens in our literature, it is mostly noted by Bionian scholars in esoteric essays that to the uninitiated or less-obsessive Bionian analyst tend to read like academic nit-picking. This book strives to take a different tack, but it cannot avoid the use of technical language that could easily be qualified as jargon to the unaccustomed ear. I have to assume, therefore, that the reader of this book has a basic level of familiarity with Bion's thought or is able to tolerate the uncertainty that comes with becoming acquainted with his language to derive some value from the ideas I am proposing. In the pages that follow, I hope to chart a clearer delineation than presently exists around one of Bion's most fascinating concepts, one that to my mind is at a point in development ripe for further clarification: *transformation in hallucinosis*.

In my years of psychoanalytic training, I have had the privilege to learn from supervisors of diverse schools of analysis, from Spotnitzian "modern" analysis, to Self-Psychologists, Lacanian, Ego-Psychological, Contemporary Freudian and Bionian. From each one of these supervisions I took something with me that I have held on to in my clinical praxis without defining myself as adhering completely to one or another of the points of view advanced. The exceptions are with the Freudian and Bionian *weltanschauungs*, which in my view, are compatible even when in tension with each other. Freud I studied deeply in undergraduate psychology in San José, Costa Rica, a program where buying a photocopy of the Spanish translation of the Laplanche-Pontalis *Language of Psychoanalysis* was a rite of passage. My interest in the work of Bion, however, began more than a decade later and through reading the papers of Thomas Ogden, Lawrence Brown, Howard Levine, and Jim Grotstein in the early to mid-aughts. But it was when the work of the Italian Field Theorists, first Antonio Ferro and later, Giuseppe Civitarese, began appearing in the *International Journal of Psychoanalysis* and then everywhere that my excitement for Bion caught fire. Additionally, in a sort of après-coup, the writing of these analysts from Pavia reacquainted me with the texts of Willie and Madeline Baranger and Enrique Pichon-Rivière, who I had encountered very early in my undergraduate psychology days in San José, but at the time lacked the experience as well as the benefit of the Italians' insights to truly comprehend. Thus, the South American connections—which later in my studies grew to include substantial contributions from Brazil—together with the North American and Italian connections, provided a framework and language I could use to have an ongoing conversation with Bion about my day-to-day clinical work.

As is true of many colleagues, it is my habit between sessions, after jotting down notes, to read psychoanalytic literature as a way of keeping my mind in tune for the next patient. The readings I turn to tend to be related to questions that are troubling me in my work. When this process evolves into writing about these questions, I am usually at a point where I feel that only in having an interested reader in mind to help me work through these questions will I be able to reach a clearer understanding and reorient myself to my patients. For me, reading and writing about psychoanalysis is always about preparing for the next analytic conversation. Over the years, the questions that have repeatedly appeared in my clinical work and hence in my readings have had to do with the nature of therapeutic action, analytic attention, and listening. These three have led me consistently to Bion's writings on *transformations* and *dreaming the session* and, to my focus here, *transformations in hallucinosis*. This concept has struck me as both clinically immensely rich and theoretically complex. An ever-growing number of papers are being written on the subject. However, as I hope to describe in these pages, there is a lack of consistency in how this concept is applied in our literature, so that the term transformation in hallucinosis is often used as an umbrella term that covers a small variety of experiences that are *functionally* different from each other. My central thesis is that the analyst's functioning, his receptivity and ability to make sense out of what is occurring between himself and the patient, and his ability to find words to represent it to them—the basic psychoanalytic task—is enhanced when the distinction between what constitutes *two basic types of hallucinosis* can be made and kept in mind. This is particularly the case when the transformations that are required in both the analyst's and patient's minds are of experiences that fall into the category of what in psychoanalysis we've termed unrepresented states. The distinction I will draw is between 1. hallucinosis that evacuates potential meaning, emerging in the crux of unrepresented internal states, into bizarre objects for the purpose of modifying the painful reality this experience puts the individual in touch with, what I will refer to as *transformations in positive hallucinosis*; and 2. hallucinosis that negativizes this meaning or the potential for making meaning, through dismantling (Meltzer, 1975), excessive evacuation, and attacks on linking for the purpose of decoupling the individual with painful reality in the service of diminishing anxiety and altering his experience. The latter I will term *transformations in negative hallucinosis*, following and extending André Green's concept of negative hallucination. In positive hallucinosis, what remain in the subject's field of experience are strange and persecutory particles that the subject reacts rather than relates to. In transformations in negative hallucinations, what remains is a blank or a negative space, a hole into which the subject's field of experience is collapsed.

In the general Bionian psychoanalytic literature, this distinction has not been formally established, though various authors—too many to list in this introduction—describe and illustrate the range of experiences covered by this term. The Janus-faced nature of hallucinosis regarding the directionality of alpha-function—for this is what is at core here—is rarely, if ever, clearly noted or spelled out. In transformations in positive hallucinosis, or T(+H),[3] on reflection the analyst can sense the remains of dream-work-alpha. Shards of meaning are preserved even as the whole is being dismantled. However, what had been a burgeoning alpha process breaks down and shifts into reverse, and the evacuated alpha-elements become de-codified into sensuous beta elements, in effect, a hallucination. In transformations in negative hallucinosis, or T(−H) the analyst becomes an unwitting participant in a fulminating reversal of alpha-functioning that is more totalizing than the one described earlier. The two, however, may often appear in tandem. T(−H) reach and effect the patient's and analyst's ability to create meaning (alpha-functioning), and in the face of this, the analyst's task is to restart this process in his own mind in order to redirect alpha-functioning toward representation. In T(+H) something "appears" without a referent to an object and is meaningless unless given meaning through the analyst's dreaming function. In T(−H) something disappears, the object and its referent, and once recognized the analyst's task is the same as in T(+H). To my mind, drawing clearer distinctions between these two functions can open the analyst's mind to what is happening in the room by narrowing and focusing his listening. Not drawing this distinction carries the risk of the analyst becoming unaware of how his dreaming and thinking processes are being compromised in the service of actualizing the patient's phantasy of the destruction of meaning, leading ultimately to acting out, impasses, premature diagnosis of un-analyzability, and the analyst's own diminished sense of competency in his work, potentially leading to a crisis in his analytic identity.

During the time of the writing of this monograph, Giuseppe Civitarese published two important papers on exactly the fine-point I am making on transformations in hallucinosis.[4] However, there are important differences in how we understand the clinical phenomenon I think we are both trying to describe. To begin with, he does not describe, as I do, what he refers to as *invisible visible hallucinations*, a term Bion used only twice and never defined, as a form of transformations in negative hallucinosis. Additionally, he clearly separates it from André Green's concept of negative hallucination, while I regard it as a form of André Green's *negative hallucination of thought*. There are also important differences in the psychical defenses that Civitarese and I theorize are involved. The differences between our two ways of thinking about what in my view amounts to the same metapsychological and clinical phenomenon will be worked out in Chapter 3.

In the chapters that follow, I will draw from Bion's theory of thinking and the development of post-Bionian authors to elucidate the two forms of hallucinosis I am proposing. Transformations in hallucinosis is a concept that goes to the heart of how Bion thinks of the psychoanalytic process. But that heart keeps expanding and transforming the work of post-Bionian analysts today, inspiring new ways of thinking about clinical problems that endure but never cease to fascinate those of us who study his work deeply. For this reason, related concepts such as dreaming, reverie, negative capability, negative hallucination of thinking, non-dreaming, the psychoanalytic field, psychoanalytic listening, ontological anxiety, the claustrum, arrogance, invisible-visible hallucinations, and other Bionian and Post-Bionian developments of recent years, central to how contemporary analysts think of the psychoanalytic process today, will also be explored.

Chapter by chapter, this book is organized thus: in Chapter 1, I will trace how the concept of transformations in negative hallucinosis relates to Wilfred Bion's experiences in the first World War. Through the analysis of various published accounts of Bion's traumatic experiences of the loss of his friends and comrades in battle, Bion's personal transformations in hallucinosis will serve to help us understand the later clinical concept. I hypothesize transformations in *negative* hallucinosis to be undergirding Bion's oft-noted hallucination of the poplar trees in a pivotal moment of his war experiences. Traces between the poplar tree negative hallucination and Bion's famous poppy fields example in his book *Transformations* are also explored.

In Chapter 2, I introduce the distinction between transformations in hallucinosis and hallucinations. Donald Meltzer's description of transformations in hallucinosis is analyzed as comprising examples of both negative and positive hallucinosis. I introduce more formally the concept of transformations in negative hallucinosis and link it with Bion's theory of thinking and André Green's depiction of negative hallucination. I then offer the case vignette of Ms. S as an illustration and discuss some technical considerations for working through a state of transformation in negative hallucinosis.

In Chapter 3, I attempt to clarify the metapsychology that underpins transformations in negative hallucinosis. Positive and negative transformations in hallucinosis are further differentiated in relation to André Green's concept of negative hallucination, including the dead mother and negative hallucination of thinking. I connect Bion's attacks on linking and Green's objectalization/disobjectalization functions and hypothesize them as taking part in transformations in negative hallucinosis. Giuseppe Civitarese's work on invisible-visible hallucinations comes into focus here, which I compare with my formulation of transformations in negative hallucinosis.

In Chapter 4, I briefly revisit the case of Ms. S (from Chapter 2) to introduce enactment as a challenging clinical implication of the phenomenon of transformations in negative hallucinosis. I add a second case, that of Mr. D, in detail to illustrate the disorienting experience of being caught in a state of chronic enactment with a psychotic patient. Mawson's ideas on ontological anxiety and Cassorla's descriptions of non-dreams-for-two come into focus, and I discuss them as lenses through which the analyst may understand his experiences with the patient and regain his analytical footing when lost. In this chapter, I also attempt to tighten the relationship between non-dreams-for-two, dreaming, and the container-contained relationship. I conclude the chapter with my idea of "finding one's ghost", a phrase that captures the analytic task of both participants to locate and reclaim the warded off and dreaded parts of their unlived lives in the other.

In Chapter 5, I discuss Bion's paper *On Arrogance* in order to describe the technical challenges posed when the analysts' interventions are considered from an intersubjective lens. I also look at the co-creation of the patient's trauma and its relationship to the O of the session, considered through the vertex of the impact of the analyst's interpretations. I introduce the extended case vignette of Ms. C to illustrate an ongoing transformation in negative hallucinosis co-created by the analytic couple and actualizing the patient's relational trauma. Mawson's ontological anxiety comes into focus again, this time in more depth as I describe the analyst's resistances to self-awareness during transformations in negative hallucinosis. The chapter ends with my discussion of André Green's conceptualization of *passion* as one of the three modalities of affect and the nature and function of representation.

In Chapter 6, I introduce the reader to Mr. W, whose case will help me illustrate Donald Meltzer's idea of the claustrum. I describe the claustrum in detail and connect it to transformations in negative hallucinosis. I then discuss the clinical implications of the claustrum through the cases of Ms. A and Ms. Q, introducing Meltzer's idea of the *aesthetic conflict*. A brief analysis of Charlotte Wells' film *Aftersun*, and the interaction between father and daughter that form the center of this beautiful film, is offered as a way of finalizing the discussion of the claustrum and its relationship to transformations in negative hallucinosis and concluding this book.

Bion's work is rich, immensely so, as well as unclear in so many ways that, to our benefit, offer us potential spaces to continue to think with and through him about our clinical experiences. Only in doing so can we truly appreciate how he dreamt, for future generations, new forms of loving, hating, knowing, and being psychoanalysis.

Notes

1 Attributed to Bion's colleague and friend A. K. Rice by Isabel Menzies Lyth (1981).
2 Marina Ferreira da Rosa Ribeiro has an interesting take on this question as it relates to Bion's concept of *reverie*. For her, the blurriness that can befall Bion's concepts is directly related to the fact of their clinical relevance and usefulness, to the point that the blurriness is a testament to their wide applicability. See Ribeiro (2022).
3 Throughout this book, I will be following Bion in using the symbols T(H) for transformation in hallucinosis and add my own modification for transformations in positive and negative hallucinosis, respectively T(+H) and T(−H).
4 See Civitarese, G. (2023) Invisible-Visual Hallucinations in Bion's "Attacks on Linking". *International Journal of Psychoanalysis* 104:197–222; Civitarese, G. & Berrini, C. (2022) On Using Bion's Concepts of Point, Line, and Linking in the Analysis of a 6-Year-Old Child. *Psychoanalytic Dialogues* 32:17–35.

Chapter 1

Transformations, or, what does a field of poppies really look like?

Poppy fields

To explore the wider subject of transformations in hallucinosis, a preliminary understanding of Bion's concept of *transformation* seems an appropriate place to start. Bion introduced into psychoanalysis a paradigm shift that involved a steady moving away from the Freudian vertex of a mind that *distorts* mental contents to diminish anxiety, toward an understanding of a mind that *transforms* mental content into ever-increasing complexity and refined contact with reality to affect growth.[1] From the start of his work on groups, through his five major books,[2] and ending in his autobiographical magnus opus, *Memoir of the Future*, Bion formulated and revised an ever finer grasp on how the mind receives and metabolizes experience for growth through the assignment of personal meaning. In Bion's view, the mind is paradoxically situated in a relationship with emotional experience[3] where, while reaching for it, it is not capable of symbolizing and assimilating its totality. That is, the mind is *stupid*[4] to emotional reality, or truth, and finds diverse forms of modulating its contact with this reality by affecting changes in the forms in which this experience is rendered. When the environment in which this experience is had supports the nurturing and development of meaning, the transformations are of the type that complexify experience through the creation of greater links with other experience, adding depth and dimension to the mind. However, when the environment is less than optimal for the containment of experience and the nurturing of meaning, transformations move in the direction of downgrading complexity by eliminating these links, taking with them sense and the ability to form meaning. The latter occurs when anxiety has become unbearable and comes at the cost of contact with emotional links to internal and external reality. Consequently, the mind's ability to breathe, to think, and to find ever expanding ways of being in the world is constrained, if not stunted or derailed. Bion's short paper, *On Arrogance*, offers an excellent description of how the mind's relationship to emotional truth and reality—what he will later call O (1965, 1970)—is always gnarled in the tension between knowing and unknowing, thinking and non-thinking, communicating, receiving, evacuating and acting out. Transformations of emotional experience are involved every step of the way.

DOI: 10.4324/9781003520740-2

In its simplest terms, a *transformation* is "turning one thing from its initial form into a new form" (IPA, 2023, p. 687); more specifically, for Bion, a psychoanalytic transformation is a "change in forms in the mind, from realization to representation" (IPA, 2023, p. 688). Bion's first formal use of the term *transformation* occurs in a small paper titled *Taming Wild Thoughts* from 1963. This paper, a precursor to his major 1965 work, *Transformations*, contains an earlier version of what in the latter book is *transformed* into what by now has become the classic example of *the field of poppies*. Both versions are interesting to render one after the other:

In *Taming Wild Thoughts*:

> If a competent artist, using the artistic conventions familiar to Western civilization, were to paint a field of poppies, we should have no difficulty in saying it was a field of poppies. Why should this be so? The lines on a straight stretch of railway would be thought of as being parallel, yet we should recognize a painting in which they were represented by lines that converged. And so on.
>
> I propose to use the term "transformation" to describe the process, whatever it is, by which the painter has transformed his experience into oil and pigment disposed on the canvas. But I don't wish the term to mean what it would mean if I said a building had been transformed by a painter or a decorator- that the field of poppies has been used as raw material for the manufacture of canvas, oil, and pigment. Nor do I mean to suggest that the observer of the painting thinks he has discovered the source of the raw material if he describes the painting as a field of poppies.
>
> (pp. 105–106)

This excerpt is taken from a long paragraph, which Bion ends with his wish that the reader understands that by *transformation*, he means the evolving form taken by "the emotional experience whose constantly conjoined elements I have represented by the term" (p. 106). Immediately after, he writes:

> As a first step towards understanding the meaning, I shall resume my discussion of my model, the field of poppies and the painting that represents it, and my "myth" that an artist has effected a transformation. The realization—i.e., the field of poppies and all the similar objects—I shall represent by the sign "O".

O, for Bion, is a sign he uses to denote ultimate reality, "the absolute fact" (1965, p. 141) or "the thing-in-itself" (idem, p. 162). A transformation is the phenomenal counterpart of "O" (ibidem). With O as its source, a transformation refers to the process a patient's experience undergoes as it changes from one state and form to another (Barahona, 2022). Everything changes, but everything also stays the same in the sense that the *invariant*—that to which the analyst's ear is attuned—remains as both a remnant and a live-wire, connecting previous transformations and establishing a line of continuity and identity between and across the different forms. The ability to effect transformations is a sign of psychic health, relatively speaking, since it involves alpha-functioning of some sort—the capacity to change sense information into units of thought (Lopez-Corvo, 2003). However, in states of ill-health, such as psychosis, transformations may be for the worse. In these cases, transformations lead to positive and negative hallucinosis, as I will further describe, where reversal of alpha-function returns psychological experience to sensual beta form, back to the thing-in-itself, to O. The problem for the psychotic, Bion writes, is that he "is unable to transform O into T" (1965, p. 162), if T represents "the total development experienced in any transformation" (Lopez-Corvo, 2003, p. 290), or its hypothetical final state.

Bion here is working out a theory of transformations that will take final form in his 1970 book, *Attention and Interpretation*, where he further develops his ideas on *transformations in O*. In this passage from *Transformations* to *Attention and Interpretation*, Bion worked through his thinking on the types of transformations that moved from realization, or O, to representation, or K, to transformations in O itself, in the fabric of felt inner reality and the experience of being. However, the trail of his evolving ideas on the matter passes through his earlier work on:

- the transformations from pre-conceptions into conceptions and then concepts
- the transformations inherent in the passage from beta to alpha-elements
- the transformative dialectic between container-contained
- the transformative dialectic between PS↔D (Bion, 1962a, 1962b, 1963, see Malin, 2021).

In his final theory, Bion describes how a transformation is constantly conjoined with what he calls invariance, the qualities of experience that, if we are talking about patients, persists intrinsically as a component of their inner state, enduring across various representations or transformations. Symptoms, dreams, behavior, and meaningful clusters of associations are all transformations of the patient's invariants. Invariants, then, "are most often emotional" and transformations in psychoanalysis aim "to help analysts recognize that emotions may be transformed into a vast array of uniquely subjective forms" (IPA, p. 687). It is this invariance that is rendered in subsequent transformations of O into the painting of the poppy field, a dream, or a hallucination, and it is through listening to this invariant that we are able to capture a glimpse, partial but vital, of the essence of the otherwise ineffable experience to which the artist was witness and that he wished to transform into a communicable experience through painting.

To reiterate, the invariant is a key feature of this process. Additionally, Bion warns us that "the term 'transformation' may mislead unless the limitations of the implications of 'form' are recognized" (1965, p. 137). Or as Sandler puts it, "something trans-forms itself but something remains the same" (2015, p. 775). Let us move now to Bion's transformation into his second description of the poppy field, from the opening of *Transformations*:

Suppose a painter sees a path through a field sown with poppies and paints it: at one end of the chain of events is the field of poppies, at the other a canvas with pigment disposed on its surface. We can recognize the latter represents the former, so I shall suppose that despite the differences between a field of poppies and a piece of canvas, despite the transformation that the artist has effected in what he saw to make it take the form of a picture, something has remained unaltered and on this something recognition depends. The elements that go to make up the unaltered aspect of the transformation I shall call invariants.

(1965, p. 1)

Bion proposes that O can represent a beta element or an emotional experience, that in turn can serve as a realization for a subsequent transformation (IPA, 2023). The term *realization*, derived from geometry, is used by Bion to denote a form of O, or, the actual fact of the total situation. For example, from an infinite set of possible painters, poppy fields, and emotional states, *this* painter, *this* poppy field, and *this* emotional state has conjoined and been made *real, realized*, into this particular O (IPA, 2023, p. 695). In this light, if we take Bion's original description of the poppy field from *Wild Thoughts* to be a transformation of an imagined previous experience of looking at the painted poppy field, the later, refined rendering in *Transformations* is an effective transformation into K—a clearer understanding and representation—of an essential, invariant part of what he was trying to convey in the original version, now part of the O from which this newer version springs. In other words, the first description in 1963 acts as a new realization for the transformation in 1965, carrying with it a historical trail of invariances transformed into two subsequent descriptions of the painting.

In Bion's theory, transformations, "emerge and evolve directly from preceding cycles, and so are recursive in nature" (ibid, p. 696), with O at the beginning and end of the transformation cycle (ibid, p. 687). As Bion intended, Sandler (2005) analogizes the situation of painting to the act of psychoanalysis. He compares two original situations (the realization, the O), for the painter the subject that he paints, i.e., the poppy field, for the analyst the experience of analyzing a patient, and says that "they are transformed in one by painting and analysis in the other, into a painting and a psychoanalytic description" (p. 769). According to Grotstein (in Mijola, 2005, pp. 1790–1791), transformations are the analyst's

attempt to help the analysand transform that part of an emotional experience of which he is unconscious into an emotional experience of which he is conscious . . . changing the form but not the fundamental nature of the invariant aspect of the emotional experience.

The effect of the interpretation on the analytic pair will create a new realization, a new O, which will serve as basis for subsequent transformations, and function as the new compass through which transcendent invariants revealing leading emotions and anxieties will come to light.

Twelve years after *Transformations*, Bion alludes in his New York lectures (1977–1978, p. 241) to the origins of the poppy field in question being Monet's 1873 painting, *Poppies*:

> The painter sees a field of poppies—which everybody has seen—and paints a picture of them. You may see a reproduction of it—it doesn't mean a thing. If you walk into the Jeux de Paumes (sic) in Paris and see the painting itself, you think: "I never saw a field of poppies until now; now I know what it looks like"—it is an emotional experience, not a report on one. How does a great painter manage to use pigments and canvas to give countless people an idea of what a field of poppies looks like?
>
> (p. 241)

For Bion, the first time he *really saw* a poppy field, then, was when he was standing in the Jeu de Paume museum gazing at Monet's masterpiece. The new O, or realization, is now Bion having an emotional experience regarding Monet's masterpiece hanging on the wall of the museum. This is what he is transforming for us now in his subsequent and varying two descriptions. In doing so, he simultaneously transmits the epistemological truism that the essence of the poppy field can never be fully captured by any one representation or transformation of its O, though the truly great painter or attentive analyst is able to apprehend something of its invariance and transform it into something *public* (Bion, 1958–1979). As already stated, the O from which this masterpiece emerges, the emotional experience of the original painter regarding that poppy field, is the source of the transformation into painting. That poppy field *exists now as if for the first time*, in both Monet at the moment of encountering it and in Bion decades later in the museum, but only because it evokes in the observer a link to a transcendental experience captured in the invariances of that O that may or may not have to do with an actual poppy field but the quality of an experience that is called forth, reaching back into the deep recesses of our individual and collective subjectivities.

Of men and poppies

In all likelihood, Bion may have contemplated the poppy field well before setting foot in Jeu de Paume, and he tells us about it in his *Memoir of the Future*:

> *Captain Bion:* I stared at the speck of mud trembling on the straw. I stared through the front flap at the clods of earth sprouting up all around us. I stared at the dirty strained face of my driver Allen—my strained face as I sat by me; at the boomerang that Allen sent me from Australia. I got out and hovered about six feet above us. I knew "they" would . . . and saw trees walking. How they walked—walk! Walk! They went like arfs arfing. Arf arf together, arfing's the stuff for me, if its not a Rolls Royce, which I'd pick out for choice. Then a nice

little Ford bright and gay, and when they came to that ford, styx I say, Valiant for S'truth passed over and all the stumpets sounded for him on the uvver side. Cooh! What 'append then? 'E talked a lot more about Jesus and dog and man and then 'e sez, all sudden like, Throw away the uvver crutch! Coo! Wot 'append then? 'E fell on 'is arse. And is Arse wuz angry and said, Get off my arse! You've done nothing but throw shit at me all yore life and now you expects England to be my booty! *Boo-ootiful soup; in a shell-hole in Flanders Fields. Legs and guts . . . must 'ave bin twenty men in here—Germ'um and frogslegs and all starts!* We didn't 'alf arf I can tell you. Let bruvverly luv continue. No one asked 'im to fall-in! No one arsed 'im to come out either—come fourth, we said and E came 5th and 'e didn't ½ stink. Full stop! E' said. The parson 'e did kum, 'e did qwat. 'E talked of Kingdom Come. King dumb come.

(1975, p. 57, my italics)

Bion's *Memoir of the Future* has confused as many as it has fascinated. As was observed by Margot Waddell (2011) and Meg Harris Williams (2010), it is a literary work. *Memoir* comprises not only a working-out of clinical insights through an emotionally interactive text (Mawson, 2014) but a creative investigation and account "of the inside story" of Bion's self-development, including the reasons he became an analyst (Waddell, 2011, p. 366). And it is not difficult to discern the autobiographical invariants in Bion's scientific writing, as many have pointed out.[5] In his late life relocation to Los Angeles from London, as well as in his metapsychology and more specifically his theory of thinking, *in itself* a theory of trauma (see Brown, 2005), a reader encounters traces of Bion's search for a way into, through, and out of the invariance of his life's trajectory. Like the master painter, he created in the process greater and richer transformations in his and our psychoanalytic experiences as people and as analysts. We in turn have been better positioned by his work to effect transformation in our patients. But the *poppiness of the poppies*, if we will, the invariance that persists throughout transformations are testimony to the aliveness of the emotions and their communicability. While not still pulsating with pain, these emotions remain palpable, pulsing through the ages, throughout one's lifetime and across the generations of the societies in which we belong, so that while manageable, they remind us of our common kinship and humanity. Also personal, every encounter with O reminds us likewise of our individuality.

If we change our vertex (Bion, 1974), we may then imagine an earlier moment of Bion *really seeing* the poppy field, perhaps while reading John McCrae's poem, *In Flanders Field* from 1918, popular during the war in which both men served.[6] "Flanders Field", where in *Memoir of the Future* he found himself in a "*boo-ootiful soup*" of "*legs and guts*" refers to the WWI battlefields in the areas between West and East Flanders, Belgium, and Nord-Pas-de-Calais, France. This is where Bion spent one and a half years of his young life, fighting as a 21-year-old tank commander on the Western Front. Here is McCrae's rendition of the time he himself spent there as a physician and a soldier:

In Flanders Fields

In Flanders Fields, the poppies blow
Between the crosses, row on row,
That mark our place; and in the sky
The larks, still bravely singing, fly
Scarce heard amid the guns below.

We are the dead. Short days ago
We lived, felt dawn, saw sunset glow,
Loved and were loved, and now we lie,
In Flanders fields

Take up our quarrel with the foe:
To you from failing hands we throw
The torch; be yours to hold it high.
If ye break faith with us who die
We shall not sleep, though poppies grow
In Flanders fields.

"If ye break faith with us who die. We shall not sleep, though poppies grow in Flanders fields". If you will not hold in your mind what happened to us, if you forget us, if we are vanished from your mind, we will remain forever awake, but the poppies that grow above us will remind you that though awake, we are not alive, not asleep, but terrified and insomniac. We can hear in these lines by McCrae something of Bion's insight into how, through the living memory of those whom we love and love us, we are transformed from an experience of inert, infinite pain into humans, people, with names and a history, links that survive us beyond the crosses that now represent us. Because alive we can sleep, because repressed and dreamt, we are no longer hallucinated.

According to at least one account of the inspiration behind this poem, McCrae wrote it in five minutes after performing the burial service for a close friend who was killed in the Battle of Ypres, where Bion also fought. McCrae noticed at this time how quickly poppies grew around the graves of those who died. A fellow soldier, who witnessed McCrae writing the poem on the back of a parked ambulance, later noted to a newspaper reporter how the poet's eyes strayed onto and around the site of his friend's grave as he wrote. After reading it, the fellow soldier told the paper that "the poem was almost an exact description of the scene in front of us both" (Regina Leader Post, 1968). We imagine here an O that is *realized* by the emotional experience of one soldier poet, McCrae, out of an infinite set of soldier poets in that battlefield, including Bion, burying and mourning his close friend, one of another infinite set of soldiers and close friends killed in that battle, while looking out at the surrounding field of poppies, one in an infinite set of fields of poppies in that war. In *In Flanders Fields*, we can read the transformation of this O that emerges, almost instantaneously, from McCrae's experience. Does this transformation in O propel some of the invariants condensed in what is a future realization, decades later, of older Bion regarding the *real poppy field* in the Jeu de Paume? Is it the ghost of his younger self that he encounters there, an "invisible-visual hallucination" (1958–1979, p. 81), in Monet's poppy field? Bion writes in *Memoir*, "I would not go near the Amiens-Roye road for fear I should meet my ghost—I died there. For though the Soul should die, the Body lives for ever" (1977b, p. 38). The body, as in McCrae's poem, does not sleep. But in the earlier excerpt from *Memoir of the Future*, Bion writes "I stared at the dirty strained face of my driver Allen—my strained face as I sat by me" (1975, p. 57). In *whose* ghost is Bion terrified to see himself, walking down the Amiens-Roye Road, cradled on both sides by infinite fields of poppies?

The three deaths of Private Sweeting

The Amiens-Roye Road is that stretch of highway extending between the towns of Amiens and Roye, around which the final stage of the war was fought. The front lines of the Western front at this time crossed this road, starting south of Amien as far as Verdun, up and arching toward the northeastern town of Arras, west of Cambrai and Bourlon Wood, and south of Ypres—all places where Bion was deployed and fought. On the 8th of August—the first day of the Allied final offensive against the Germans and the day he "died"—Bion and his men were heading south toward German lines with the aim of eventually making it back toward Berles-au-Bois, some 50 kilometers from Amiens, amidst a barrage of enemy artillery fire and a combination of dense fog and thick black smoke that impeded their ability to see as far their own hands. Then Bion suffered an experience that would haunt him in the form of his ghost walking down the Amiens-Roye Road awaiting his return 57 years later to write about it in his *Memoir of the Future.*

Bion tells us three versions of this same event, where in each version something stays the same and something has changed. His first narration is in his *War Memoirs* (1997), written to his parents just after demobilization, and presumably from memory since he had lost his war diary (p. 13). In remarkable detail, Bion describes his actions as well as those of the men he commanded, some of whom were his good friends, and most of whom did not survive that final engagement. As a 21-year-old tank commander, he had already lived through the battles of Bourlon Wood, Cambrai, and Ypres, among others, before enduring the final Allied assault against the Germans in the Battle of Amiens, in which once again he sent friends and comrades in tanks toward the thundering firewall of the front line. The event in question, and that Bion endeavors to represent three separate times in writing, concerned the death of Private Sweeting, a tank gunner and a runner who volunteered to follow Bion as they walked as light infantry behind the tank column he commanded while heading toward enemy lines. Much has been written about Sweeting's horrific death, and an in-depth comparison of the three different transformations into which Bion pours the O of this experience has already been accomplished by Dominic Angeloch (2021), so I will not attempt to do that here. I will instead focus on what I feel have been overlooked elements in these accounts that strike me as crucial and relate to early examples in Bion's writings of what he, decades later, will think of as *transformations in hallucinosis*. First some context.

The death of Private Sweeting is retold three times, first in his *War Memoirs*, as I previously explained, and then in 1958 as an addendum to that account called *Amiens*, written after traveling 40 years later with his wife Francesca to that French city on the boundary of what had been the Western Front. His final attempt was in his autobiographical *The Long Weekend*, in 1982.[7] In each one of these narrations, the context is more or less the same: in the pre-dawn hours of day 1 of the Battle of Amiens, August 8, 1918, Bion sent 2–5 tanks to face the enemy lines, while he and 2–4 others followed on foot. Only a few minutes after launching, one of the tanks breaks down but then starts up again. Minutes later, the enemy's response to the initial Allied volley of fire that served as cover for the tanks and infantry is overwhelming: "Their fire was so terrific that it seemed impossible to go on. We could see absolutely nothing" (1997, p. 131); "Never have I known a bombardment like this, never, never—" (ibid, p. 254).

Next, Bion is in a shell-hole with Sweeting, who was "quite a young boy and was terrified" (p. 131).[8] Sweeting is burying himself as deep into the walls of the shell-hole as he is into Bion's side for protection. Bion, in all three accounts, is dazed and trying to think of what to do next: to leave the shell-hole would mean certain death, as all the enemy fire was concentrated on where they were. To stay also meant certain death. In the midst of this, Bion enters into a state of quasi-panic when he thinks he sees the Amien-Roye Road *behind* him, when it should be to his left. He imagines this by confusing several blades of tall grass a few yards away with the tall poplar trees that line the edge of that road, as he turns around to gain his bearings. Anxiety floods Bion as he draws the tragic conclusion: he must have made a mistake with his compass bearings, and as such, sent his tanks, the men in them, himself, and Sweeting, in the wrong direction, essentially, sitting ducks parading parallel to the enemy lines, rather than charging into them in attack. As he is trying to think, seconds later, he hears Sweeting calling to him. He turns to listen closer and sees that the left side of Sweeting's chest has been blown away. In his final moments, Sweeting is asking Bion what has happened to him.

"Sir! Sir, why can't I cough?"

> What a question! What a time. . . . I looked at his chest. His tunic was torn. No, it was not his tunic; the left side of his chest was missing. He tried to look. I stopped him. I found his field dressing and pretended to fix it across the gap. And then he saw, under his left arm. . . . He sank back as if relieved, then started on a new tack.
>
> (Bion, 1982, pp. 279–280)

Deducing the gravity of the situation from Bion's stupefied response, as well as from viewing his own wound, Sweeting now implores Bion to write his mother and inform her of his death.

I will not reproduce here more text of these accounts and will only refer the reader to the heart and gut-wrenching originals. Angeloch (2021) feels that the last of the three deaths of Private Sweeting, the one contained in *The Long Weekend*, is the most compelling. In his opinion, it is the one that shows most successfully Bion's emotional growth and transformation and allows him "to find an expression for what had *really* happened" (p. 42, italics mine). He explains that only here, in this version written 60 years after the original events, is Bion able to transform the coldness and cynicism Angeloch reads in the previous two transformations into a deep sense of meaningful sadness. He draws on unexplained omissions and inclusions from one version to the next, and indeed, these stand in contrast to each other, showing an evolution in the way Bion, at first only a year later, is able to express—in other words metabolize, and finally symbolize—the horror and the terror of the experience of *that* 20-year-old Wilfred, with *that* 18-year-old Sweeting, in *that* shell-hole, in *that* bombardment, during *those* minutes of *that* war in *that* portion of Flanders Field. These transformations stand in contrast to those *that* 60-year-old Wilfred was able to reach in *that* train with *that* Francesca some 40 years later, en route to *that* Amiens, through *those* Flanders Fields, where they are able to perceive the traces—we might say negative hallucinations—of the shell-holes still remaining, covered now by weeds barely able to conceal what peered from underneath. Indeed, Bion remarks in his forward to *Amiens* how, if it seemed during the war that the barren and burnt earth was covered quickly by weed, after the war the weed stopped growing, as if giving up on its job of patching over the gaping wounds of the earth—but this is my interpretation now of attacks on linking preventing healing from trauma. These gaping wounds, however, necessitated more elaboration, and 20 years after *Amiens*, at around the age of 80 and now living in Los Angeles, *that* Bion makes his final attempt at transforming into a grievable loss what had continued to burn a shell-hole into his very being. Angeloch notes that only in this last transformation from *The Long Weekend* is the undead Sweeting given a tomb. We can deduce from Bion's writings that this epithet of representation facilitated the process of alphabetization and forgetting so necessary for the work of mourning and the work of the negative (Green, 1999b), and for the body to die so the soul might live forever:[9]

> And then I think he died. Or perhaps it was only me. I handed him over to some infantry. "Sweeting, I have to go now—to the other tanks . . .". Thank God he was paying no attention to my drivel. Two men, one on either side, draped his arms over their shoulders and stumbled along with him to the casualty clearing station. Sweeting. Gunner. Tank Corps. Died of Wounds. That, for him, was the end.
>
> (1982, p. 281)

When poppies grow, do they become poplars?

At this point, I invite the reader to follow me down an imaginative conjecture that I think will further my illustration of what Bion meant by *transformation*. It is not surprising to me that Sweeting's horrific death, and the guilty aftermath it unleashed in Bion's soul, has been the subject of much educated speculation on the traumatic origin of his thinking. Although most of the writers who trace these to his war experiences do not limit themselves to the account of Sweeting's death, the latter certainly features as an emotional climax in most accounts. It surprises me, however, how little attention has been paid to Bion's hallucination of the poplar trees on the Amiens-Roye Road, an element in the telling of the story that, while mentioned by Bion and commentators in all three transformations of Sweeting's death, is never examined in and of itself. Sweeting's death and the vision of the line of poplars trees along the Amiens-Roye Road are among the constant features of the three narratives. In all versions, Bion's attention is drawn to these two events: the vision of the poplar trees behind him, signaling his having made a grave mistake, and Sweeting's voice and finally body calling out to him in the last moments of life. Certain other occurrences that do change from scene to scene have been noted by various authors, Angeloch in particular, and have been interpreted in the context of Bion's growing capacity for containing and transforming his emotions around these events throughout his life. For instance, one might infer that the progressively larger appearance of dialogue between the two men in the shell-hole from the first to the third of the Sweeting narratives corresponds with an expansion of the container-contained capacity around the growing emotional intensity and Bion's ability to "think" it. Still, other changing features of the story stay on the periphery in commentary by other writers, and not constantly conjoined as elements that frame thoughts and emotions, obscured I think by the impact of Sweeting's agony though perhaps also absorbed by it. I think focusing on these periphery elements now, in relation to the hallucination of the poplar trees and Sweeting's death, as opposed to isolating the latter in the narrative, might offer another vertex from which to imagine the man Bion himself, as well as further illustrate his concept of *transformations* and *transformations in hallucinosis*.

The first death of Private Sweeting

Let us keep in mind that the three deaths of Private Sweeting all occur within the first few minutes on the Battle of Amiens, on August 8, 1918. This scene, in all three narrations, begins with the moments before the tanks start off into action. If we move chronologically through the three texts we see that:

In the *War Memoirs* (1997), just as they start off,

- Bion is irritated that he is asked to provide the compass readings for the line-ups of all tanks, after the commanding officer shirks the responsibility and runs away before the battle starts. From the statement, "as it turned out subsequently, these positions were correct" (p. 128), we may infer that Bion was nervous about the tanks taking direction from his possibly incorrect readings.
- At zero hour, the offensive begins, and there are four men on foot with Bion: Johnson, his close friend Hauser, the "runner" Sweeting, and another "runner". They are walking behind the tanks.

- Bion has sent off at least three tanks in front of them, containing three separate crews. These include at least, in one tank: Richards, who was a young boy sent in at the last minute to replace the previous tank commander who was arrested for looting; in another, Cartwright and O'Toole, men from Bion's original battalion who he knew well; and finally, his closest friend Asser commanding a third tank.
- A few minutes after starting, Asser's tank breaks down. Bion and the others "stood and waited for him to go on" (p. 129). Moments later, Asser's tank starts up again and continues forward.
- Just before or at the same time as taking cover *under a road bank*, and under the extreme pressure of the barrage of enemy fire that has opened up in response to the initial British and Allied volley, Bion has a hallucination where he sees a row of poplar trees in a line behind him, indicating the location of the Amiens-Roye Road. This hallucination is shared by Hauser who is next to him. In this account, they seem curious about their confusion, but otherwise unperturbed.
- Moments later, Bion and Hauser are joined by Johnson, who soon after is hit in the arm by shrapnel and retreats to the medical station. There is no mention of Sweeting being with them under the road bank.
- Seconds later, it is only Sweeting and Bion "crouched together in one spot" (p. 131). Sweeting is mortally wounded by shrapnel. We infer a few sentences later that Hauser, who becomes nauseous, was a witness to this first death of Sweeting.
- Bion has the mortally wounded Sweeting taken to the medical station by the "other runner".
- After emerging from this scene, Hauser leaves and Bion continues forward, running into Richards' broken-down tank, with Richards alive, and then Cartwright's and O'Toole's destroyed tank, with no survivors.

Two days later, at 2 am on August 10th, Bion is woken up from under his tank and given orders to turn over Asser's and Richards' two tanks to a Capt. Llewellyn to reinforce C Company who had failed to complete their objectives against the enemy. These tanks were not meant to fight that day but for this failure in the advance, and Bion and Asser were both taken aback at the unexpected news. At 4 am, they were meant to accompany Hauser's two tanks, along with two others from another section, so six in all, into battle. Not wanting Asser and his men to go into battle without him, Bion resisted and challenged the captain, proclaiming that he was less tired than Llewellyn and should therefore be the one to command his own men. This was to no avail, and Bion had no recourse but to try to cheer up Asser, who, Bion noted, didn't really need cheering up and who seemed to be doing the same for Bion by telling him "it was all in the game, and one couldn't grumble about having to fight" (p. 137). Reluctantly, Bion saw his dear friend off along with his men and reported back to headquarters, where he immediately fell asleep. Later in the evening, news reached him that this new offensive had failed. Five tanks were found destroyed with few survivors, and Richards was badly wounded.

Asser's tank, however, had disappeared. The next morning, on August 11th, the last day of the Battle of Amiens, Bion and Cook headed out in search of Asser. Bion discovered the five tanks, lined up next to each other, each exploded "like burst toads" (p. 141). But it was Cook who, having gone off on his own, returned an hour later with news of Asser, found lying next to his tank with a bullet in his heart. His crew had been taken prisoner, but it seemed Asser had refused to surrender to the German troops who captured him.

In these *War Memoirs*, Bion is recreating, in the style of a daily journal, an account for his mother of his year and a half at war. He is understandably reserved if we consider his intended audience, if not emotionally constrained by the shock of battle. The three deaths of Private Sweeting form the emotional center, a transformation in three stages of the undigested facts of Bion's agonizing experiences, throughout the war but especially the four-day Battle of Amiens that marked the beginning of the end. The account of these four days begins, in *War Memoirs*, with a few stripped-down statements masking Bion's nervousness about possibly making a fateful mistake—leading his tanks in the wrong direction based on incorrect readings (p. 128)—and end on the final day of the battle with his best friend, Asser's, courageous death (p. 139). His friend meets his tragic end after the tank he commands strays in the wrong direction, and tragically, the supporting infantry of the 52nd Division, frozen in panic, fails to rise out of their trenches to support their tanks, giving free range to the German field gun that destroyed the tanks. Considering that the other five tanks that did not stray were also destroyed, and the fact that Bion's anxieties about his compass readings occurred four days earlier, there is no obvious connection, unless unconscious, between Bion's misgivings about his compass bearings and his friend's demise. However, Bion was compelled to walk in the opposite direction after Llewellyn gave Asser his orders. If we add to this the account of the infantry's freeze response, which contributed directly to all tanks except Asser's being overwhelmed, as well as Bion's anxiousness about Asser's tank being ordered to leave without him, we might intuit an anxious link between the frozen infantry and Bion's repeated claim, in all his autobiographical writings, that he was a coward (Grotstein, 1998) who survived his friends only because the war ran out of time. Did Bion feel like he was the frozen infantry sitting back while Asser's tank moved forward to certain death? Additionally, his misgivings about the direction in which he was sending his troops on August 8th and the fact of Asser's having gone astray three days later suggest to me a link in Bion's mind composed of guilt for sending his friend "in the wrong direction" and alone toward death.

The second death of Private Sweeting

If we move now to the second death of Private Sweeting, this time recounted in *Amiens*, his addendum to the *War Memoirs* written 40 years later, we see that:

- Major de Freine angrily orders Bion to extend the compass readings of his own section to cover all the tank sections. Bion is unsure he will be able to do this properly, and feels burdened, angry, and depressed (pp. 246–247). Major Morgan a few moments later is nervous about the readings, and Bion finds this a silly question.

- At zero hour, the tanks begin moving, with Bion inside Asser's tank. He promptly exits and, with Sweeting in tow, watches the tank disappear into the wall of fog and smoke.
- After Bion leaves Asser's tank, there is only one other person with Bion: Sweeting.
  There is no mention of Hauser, Johnson, or the other runner.
- Suddenly, a tank breaks down in front of Bion. It is not Asser's, as in the previous telling, but the one containing Cartwright and O'Toole, his friends from his original battalion. Bion is now inside *this* tank coaching the young, panicking Corporal Stone on how to start the engine again, including the delicate, sensitive task of changing the filter in the midst of the overwhelming barrage of shell-fire shaking the tank: "Think, Corporal, think . . . Corporal Stone, keep awake. . . . My God, are these tanks made out of jelly? . . . Tap the sides of the container gently with the knuckle. . . . Listen, Corporal, listen." (pp. 251–252).
- Having helped Corporal Stone start the tank up again, Bion drops out the back hatch, only to watch, moments later, the same tank take a direct hit, killing Stone, Cartwright, and O'Toole instantly. "A sheet of flame shot above it . . . suddenly its sides seemed to open *like a flower*" (p. 252, my italics).
- Bion now reaches down and touches a metal track that he notices next to them, as if trying to understand where they are on the terrain, and seconds later both he and Sweeting jump into a shell-hole to take cover. In the onslaught of gunfire, Bion becomes consumed in trying to bear in mind the next steps of the plan, which are to meet up with Asser's tank at "Berle au Bois".
- In the midst of the intense bombardment and confusion, Bion turns around and sees behind him the line of poplar trees that align the Amiens-Roye Road: "What could it possibly mean? This long straight line of trees?" (p. 253). This line of trees should be to his left, not directly behind him. Bion is now flooded with anxiety as it dawns on him that he must have indeed gotten his compass bearings wrong and sent his tanks and himself and Sweeting in the wrong direction.
- Almost simultaneously, Sweeting is hit by a shell. Bion can barely think as Sweeting is now asking him what has happened, calling out for his mother, and then repeating over and over his mother's address. Bion is near the point of insanity:

Never have I known bombardment like this, never, never—Mother, Mother, Mother—never have I known a bombardment like this, he thought. I wish he would shut up. I wish he would die. Why can't he die? Surely he can't go on living with a great hole torn in his side like that (p. 254).

The chapter containing the second death of Private Sweeting ends here, but *Amiens* continues for 50 more pages before ending suddenly in mid-sentence and in mid conversation with Major de Freine, who is lauding Bion for his steeled nerve and not yet having lost his mind. The two have just discussed how they suspected O'Toole had suffered a nervous breakdown around the time he was killed due to his having seen too much continuous action. Says de Freine, "Well, for that matter, so have you, but you don't show any signs of cracking up, I'm glad to say". Bion begins to respond, but instead of finishing what he was going to say, ends the book. In the introduction to *Amiens*, Francesca Bion explains that Bion put this text down here at this point and never finished it because he needed to turn to other pressing projects, most notably *Learning from Experience*. However, it is notable to me that what would have followed in the sequence of events, had Bion finished describing to de Freine just how wrong he was for believing him brave, is the account of Asser's death. The last mention of Asser occurs just four pages earlier, when his friend's tank was still lost: "I wish I'd found Asser, all the same; I'd like to know what has happened to him" (p. 301).

The third death of Private Sweeting

In *The Long Weekend* (1982), Bion writes how a day before the Battle of Amiens is to begin, Sergeant O'Toole, who had been Bion's tank sergeant at the start of the war and part of his original crew, pulls him aside and confesses to wanting to die:

> Sir, I don't want anything more. I don't mean I want to be invalidated out—no shell-shock for me. But this time sir, I feel I want six feet of earth and nothing else. I know its got to happen; I feel it in my bones, sir. Will you write to my people, sir?
>
> (p. 268)

This is what Bion and Major de Freine had referred to in *Amiens* when discussing O'Toole's loss of nerve. As the company commander, Bion was entrusted to write the fathers and mothers of those in his unit who were killed in action: "Sir, will you write to my mother, sir? Will you write to my people, sir?"

The day before the battle, Bion lies down on the cold, hard ground to fall asleep, and has a nightmare, "grey, shapeless; horror and dread gripped me" (1982, p. 269). The dream is about going into battle, and Bion wakes in time to prepare for the real thing.

> Yet for a moment I wished it was only a dream. In the dream I must have wished it was only a war.
>
> (ibidem)

A few pages earlier, the mood had been quite different, and here is where we first learn, in this text, of Asser, a young man a year younger than Bion and around 19 years old. Asser is cheerful and patriotic, reminding Bion of what he and his friends were like back in England before the war. It had also only been a week since Asser joined their company, but in what, in war, must feel like an existence that defies linear time, they had become close, and Bion asked Asser to be the one to write *his* mother in the event of his death. Bion had also asked him to be next in command should he be killed, which to my mind suggests something of an important identification with this young man who he had only just met. Asser to Bion was a romantic figure, fiery, studious in appearance, whose adored brother and father, both even "more romantically shadowy figures" had been killed in action at the start of the war (p. 266–267). If Bion felt himself to be a coward, the exact opposite was true of his regard for Asser.[10]

On the night of August 7th, Bion meets his fellow British, French, and Canadian officers at headquarters to discuss the coming offensive. Bion receives his orders, which involve rebuilding a bridge over the Luce River and taking compass measurements for the tanks. With this as prologue, we may enter now into the moments before and after the third death of Private Sweeting:

- After rebuilding the bridge over the Luce River with his men, Bion is met by another tank commander and friend, Carter, who informs him that the Amiens-Roye Road will be on his left as he advances at dawn. He says to Bion, "It is lined with poplars, so you can see its direction and check your own by it" (p. 273).
- After being engulfed by an impermeably dense fog, Bion now becomes aware that this is due to there being no water in the river over which he and his men have just built the bridge. He begins to get anxious, wondering why, if he had already known the river was dry, he hadn't predicted the fog (the evaporated water) and reported it to headquarters. He tells Hauser he is worried about his tanks losing their direction in the fog. Out of a mix of anxiety and following orders, he takes out his compass and begins to take measurements.
- Bion describes something akin to the reversal of alpha-functioning in the way he begins to lose faith in his compass bearings, which he is taking as the first tank begins to line up next to him and as the enemy, hearing the engines, has started sporadically firing. Staring at his markings and at his compass, he cannot grasp what the figures of the compass bearings have to do with direction on the ground. His anxiety grows as other tanks begin to line up next to each other, all taking a cue from his own dubious markings. It is late in the evening, and the tanks idle until zero hour—crack of dawn on August 8th.
- Hours later, Bion "watche(s) the minute hand motionless, creeping, rushing headlong to zero hour", and reflects that his mother will soon be receiving a letter announcing his death. The engines pulsate, the great wall of fog is suddenly illuminated by the blinding flashes of the Allied guns, and the air above them screams demented and roaring, as Bion and two men—the brothers Sweeting—run behind the tanks. This is the first time in the three autobiographies that the second runner is identified as Sweeting's *brother*.
- Bion and the brothers Sweeting are now running "nowhere in particular", only "getting away". The enemy responds with their own volley of fire. Sweeting

screams out, "My brother!" (p. 278) as the latter disappears "complete(ly)" (idem).[11]

- Immediately after, Bion and Sweeting are in a shell-hole. Bion "tries to think" of the next steps of the plan at the same time as he is fighting off the agonizing intrusive doubt he is feeling over having sought shelter with Sweeting in this shell-hole, which only made the dread of moving more real by offering only illusory refuge from the engulfing fire.
- Trying to determine their precise location through the fog, Bion hears Carter's words in his mind as he sees the poplar trees lining the Amiens-Roye Road *behind him*, not to his left. His momentary relief at situating himself on the terrain suddenly gives way to panic as he realizes the implications.
- Now Sweeting has been hit and is trying to speak to him.

Bion's account that follows these events implies that Sweeting dies moments, maybe minutes later after the fog and fire of the initial barrage of the Allied advance passes, and Bion is able to exit the shell-hole and carry his runner over to the infantry to take him to the medical unit.[12] Advancing now, apparently alone, he runs into Cartwright's and O'Toole's destroyed tank, and "the last of Sergeant O'Toole" (p. 282). The next eight or so pages chronical two times that Bion is looking for Asser—perhaps *his* "brother" who has "disappeared completely"—finding him first at Berle au Bois, but then losing him again after sending him off on another mission with four other tank crews. In *The Long Weekend*, there are four tanks (rather than the five in *Amiens*) and Asser's. Additionally, in this account, Asser is sent off to back up the French at least a few hours *before* the other four, which depart with Bion and Hauser in tow as light infantry. In *War Diaries*, all tanks leave together without Bion, and in *Amiens*, we do not know what happened because Bion cuts his account short just as we are about to find out. Bion's narration of the moments before Asser drives off with his crew are poignant if not tender, emanating sorrow and guilt, as he describes how he has to wake the young crew up, including their commander, Asser, who have all fallen completely asleep from exhaustion. Bion tries to rouse Asser from his slumber as he is giving him his orders, and then the two go on to wake the rest of the men. As they begin to move, Bion is seized by the fear, which he does not tell Asser, that the crew will soon again fall asleep as they enter their warm tanks and drive off at 4:30 in the morning into the distance and into battle.

Bion could not but follow the nonsensical orders he was given and that in turn, had to give to Asser and the rest of his men. He could see no reasonable military advantage to launching himself and the other four tanks at what seemed like a randomly chosen 10:30 am, hours after Asser's departure. This meant they would not accompany the latter's tanks, and they themselves would not have the cover of the early morning darkness, nor, for some unexplained reason, smoke screens. In this narration of what happens next, "Richards" from the *War Memoirs* is transformed into Robertson, who is the tank commander of one of the four vehicles, and what follows occurs on August 11th, the last official day of the Battle of Amiens.

As they follow on foot behind their tanks, Bion and Hauser become suddenly alarmed when they see that the infantry that is supposed to be supporting them is neither leaving the trenches nor firing. Both men run back to the trenches and beg the officers and the colonel in command to order their troops into action, but find them all paralyzed with fear, "almost demented" and "sleepwalking" (p. 285). Desperate, Bion and Hauser turn toward the field of battle only to witness their four tanks, now way off in the distance, picked off one by one, all direct hits. In this telling, Richards/Robertson does not survive, nor do any of the crew members of the four tanks. Bion describes what he saw:

The tanks rolled up a gentle grassy slope. There was a soft muffled explosion. Roberston's tank opened *as a flower* in a nature film might unfold. Another thud; then two almost simultaneous followed. The whole four had *flowered*.

(p. 286, my italics)

Demoralized, shocked, fascinated, horrified, nearly insane, Bion and Hauser sit down to write letters.

There were now only five tank commanders left alive, or maybe six?—"there was Asser too of course. That would be more still unless something had happened to him" (p. 286). Cook, one of the remaining five, tells Bion he is going off to look for his friend. In *The Long Weekend*, there is only one moment where Bion ever mentions anything remotely close to crying, and it is when Cook returns with the news:

What I said was, "Oh". Then I burst into tears.

(p. 287)

Almost instantly, Bion pulls himself together and tells Cook he needs to write Asser's mother and simultaneously remembers he has not yet written to *Sweeting's* mother. Bion's thoughts swirl from imagining what the latter's mother might be like, to the images in his mind of the tanks bursting into flames, "like *blossoms* greeting the sun" (p. 288, my italics). Minutes earlier, it was Bion himself that had been "bursting" into tears. Now he is thinking about Sweeting's mother. Is she "a rather nice woman" or does she have "angry eyes?" Perhaps he is yearning for a "rather nice" container to transform the bursting flames of his uncontained tears. Perhaps the "angry eyes" are the sign of an ego-destructive superego that shatters the container with guilt. And perhaps this guilt makes it impossible for Bion to represent in the moment, what years and decades later he transforms into these three written accounts of Sweeting's death and all its orbiting catastrophes. Sado-erotic fascination, containing within it residues of powerlessness and sorrow, is among the transformed flames when further down in the previous paragraph he likens to copulation the sight of two slowly moving, destroyed tanks clawing up against each other. Forms of copulation, blossoms and slowly bursting flowers, emerging from the soil fertilized by the blood of his friends. Perhaps a fusion or attempt at fusion of life and death drives in the images of a tank "opening as a flower in a nature film might unfold" (ibid). Images photographed by the mind, negativized, regenerated, linking together, between flames shooting upward, recast as blossoming flowers, recast again as red poppies, perhaps again recast as poplar trees. Here I am leading up to the invariance between transformations that I sense existed for Bion between his fallen comrades in their tanks, the flowers, the blossoms of red poppies in the fields, and finally the poplar trees that lined the fateful road spanning, on one plane, the distance between Amiens and Roye, and on another the distance between Bion and his sense of integrity and sanity. In this manner, within transformations, alpha-function makes use of the Freudian primary processes[13] of displacement and condensation, or put another way, metaphor and metonymy, in transferring emotional content from one form to another, through visual and acoustic links: tall blades of grass and "trees walking"; poplar trees, men and poppies; bright red flames shooting up, "flowering" tanks and blossoming flowers; tanks bursting and Bion bursting into tears in a field of poppies.

Bion writes Sweeting's mother her letter:

Dear Madame, I am sorry I have not been able to write to you before about the death of your son. He was a good lad and you must have been a very good mother to him. I was with him at the end when he knew he was dying. You were the person who was in his mind in those last hours and it was your name that was on his lips. I hope you will feel proud that he loved you so much. I am, dear Madame, his officer that day.

And the letter ends there, mid-sentence (p. 288).

Poppies and poplars

To repeat, what are we to make out of all these flowering tanks, blossoms, and poplar trees? And what do these, if anything, say about what a field of poppies *really* looks like? My sense, when reading the three autobiographies in the light of Bion's theory of transformations, is that what Rycroft (1995) might have simply called an *illusion*, more definable in old psychological language as "a subjective perversion of the objective content" (p. 77), today in Bion's language we might call a *transformation in hallucinosis*. Far from a simple misperception based on wish fulfillment, I contend that Bion is describing having had a waking dream that he *could not* dream because he could not think through the overwhelming terror he was experiencing. This emotional experience, that could not be dreamt, is endured as if in the absence of an outer shell to contain it, the *caesura* lining both the inner and outer folds of the experience shattered, so that the emotional agony that Bion carries with him before entering the shell-hole and extending throughout his life, his emotional truth of being a guilty coward, traverses the caesura and is hallucinated before his eyes as a way of managing the overwhelming experience. This occurs when the devastating fear is divested of any representation by an overwhelmed ego and negatively transformed into nameless dread. Existing now as unrepresented infinite dread, Bion unsees the road he traveled in external reality and sees the road he traveled in emotional reality. In other words, Bion negatively hallucinated the correct path he and Sweeting were coming from—his senses could not make sense of what was before him—and positively halluci- nated the poplar trees and the incorrect path in its place—his senses projected before him what was inside of him. Hallucinating that the Amiens-Roye Road was *behind him* and not to his left, psychically certified to him that in his incom- petence he was steering his men toward certain death. We can read in his obses- sive account of the compass bearings that there is always someone, either Bion, or another (internal) officer, doubting his capacity to think straight about how to direct the tanks. And already, in his confusion over the relationship between the figures on the compass and direction on the ground, we can witness the beginning formation of bizarre objects, indicating a process of reversal of alpha-functioning under the stress of the upcoming battle, and paving the way for transformations in hallucinosis. Both the (+) *and* (−) transformations in hallucinosis concretized for Bion his deepest feeling of inadequacy. Note that they did not *represent* the inadequacy, but instead made it *real*; they *realized* the inadequacy into a *fact*, a new O, from which there was no way forward but through the writing of the three narratives. Because his conviction of cowardice was such an *undigested fact*, as plain as daylight to him, he could not dream the poplars into being merely a misperception of the tall blades of grass standing in for his deepest fears about himself. That he turned out to be correct in his compass readings probably offered only short-lived relief, as one disaster after another befell him and his men, end- ing in the heroic death of his closest friend in the war, and in a very true sense in his own death.

After the Battle of Amiens, Bion is on home leave in England, inside a Turkish bath. Lying in the water, he experiences something in between an awake and an asleep dream, what he would later refer to as a hallucination in sleep. He tells us of his hallucinated thoughts process:

> "Mother, mother. You will write to my mother sir, won't you?" "No, blast you, I shan't! Shut up! Can't you see I don't want to be disturbed?" These old ghosts, they never die. They don't even fade away; they preserve their youth wonder- fully. . . . The Turkish bath was very refreshing; I felt so clean. It's not real, you know; just kind of a trick. Really, of course, everyone stinks. They have a way of making people look so life-like, but really, we are dead. I? Oh yes, I died—on August 8th 1918.
>
> (pp. 295–296)

Bion knew "these old ghosts", among them Sweeting, Sweeting's brother, Cart- wright, Corporal Stone, O'Toole, Richards/Robertson, and finally and most impor- tantly Asser, would never be transformed from their state of beta elements in his mind, undigested sorrow and horror, and that as long as this was the case he would remain identified with them, those for whose deaths he felt personally responsible, if not for his actions then for his inability to die heroically and thus not abandon them. These old ghosts both "never die", but they preserve their youth "wonderfully", or, in the words of Binyon, "Age shall not weary them, nor the years condemn". We know that Bion was familiar with Binyon's poem from 1914 because he mentions it in the final lines of the prologue to *Amien*:

> There were not many of those ("men of splendid minds") left by 1918, and yet there were some. I remember Asser—Asser, who was only nineteen and who joined our battalion with all the freshness, enthusiasm and youthful belief that he was joining in some wonderful and glorious adventure. He did not grow old, "as we who are left grow old" [Laurence Binyon, "For the Fallen"].
>
> (1997, p. 216)

My impression from reading all three autobiographies is that the Amiens-Roye Road incident where Bion "saw" the tall poplar trees lining the road and unsaw reality was a first transformation, in this case into hallucinosis, of the terror, shame, and guilt he felt as the destruction was happening all around him and as he was ordered and similarly ordered his men into action and death. But Bion's pain being infinite, that is, too great to be contained in a mind that at this point was shattered, he continued and indeed struggled all of his life to transform it, into transformations of higher, more complex forms, with varying degrees of success, and the shape and form of these transformations were these three memoirs and his later *Memoir of the Future*.[14] Moreover, the transformations continued to unfold throughout his ever evolving theories of mind, ultimately leading to the work *Transformations* itself, and finally, to a concept that would help him, and psychoanalysts after him, understand the source of transformations, both their wellspring and their realization, the concept of "O" in *Attention and Interpretation*. The invariants throughout these works and his life are the qualities of deep guilt and shame, terror, sorrow and regret.

Grotstein (1998) wonders if in his admiration for Asser, Bion identified with him in an attempt "to undo the coward" he felt himself to be. For Grotstein, it was possible that Bion's statement that he too had died contained a confession of his survival guilt (p. 612). This is very plausible. Interestingly, Grotstein, himself Bion's analysand, gets the date of Asser's death wrong, placing it on August 7th (p. 612), exactly one day before the Battle of Amiens had even started. Did Grotstein here transform into hallucinosis the wrong date of Asser's death, in identification with his beloved analyst, in order to undo Bion's persecutory feelings of cowardice and guilt by taking Asser out of that battle all together? Curiously, Grotstein's transformation in hallucinosis, if we may call it that, does not stop here. He writes,

> It was the death of Asser, and how Asser died, that caused Bion to state, "I died on August 7th on the Amiens-Roye Road".
>
> (Grotstein, 1998, p. 612)

But Bion never said that. He said, as we read in the previously cited nightmare in the Turkish bath, "Oh yes, I died—on August 8th 1918" (1982, p. 296), ending this sentence after the date. Might we think that Grotstein too has identified Bion with Asser, so that neither of them even made it to the real battle, both dying together before the fighting begins? Grotstein then refers to the Battle of Amiens as the *Battle of the Amiens-Roye Road*, being the only writer, from what I can tell, to refer to it in this way, and later adds, as I already mentioned, that Asser's death was in this (hallucinated) *Battle of the Amiens-Roye Road*, the day before the real Battle of Amiens began, and three days before the real Asser was killed. Might Grotstein be creating an alternative reality through the evacuated and fragmented remains of the unbearable "O" that was Bion's anguish in the actual Battle of Amiens? In this way, did Grotstein place a negatively hallucinated Asser on the Amiens-Roye *Road*, where the poplar trees grow tall, far away from the place and time where the real Asser died alone, and in Bion's conscience abandoned by him? Bion said he would not go near this road of hallucinated horror for fear of meeting his ghost (1977b, p. 38). Who else, apart from himself, might Bion meet there, if not Asser?

And finally, what do flowering tanks, blossoms, and poplar trees have to do, if anything, with what a real poppy field looks like, unless poppy fields are a final transformation, a realization, the "O" of those very same poplar trees aligning that fateful road, the "blades of tall grass" in themselves a transformation of Bion's comrades and Asser, had they been given more time and shown more mercy to have been allowed to grow tall and old?

Notes

1 I am aware that this is an oversimplification of Freud's theory of mind, which involves several converging principles of psychic functioning. Readers should refer to Civitarese, 2023a, pp. 10–31 for a more nuanced discussion of this perspective.

2 These are *Learning from Experience* (1962a), *Elements of Psychoanalysis* (1963), *Second Thoughts* (1964), *Transformations* (1965), and *Attention and Interpretation* (1970).

3 In this and the chapters that follow, I will use the term emotional experience, and variants of this, i.e., inner experience, etc., all admittedly ambiguous terms, to refer to what in psychoanalysis we simply refer to as psychic reality. This is for the sake of variation in the writing, but it is well to define what is meant by these terms in general. For Bion, *psychic reality* is equivalent to what is felt to be emotionally true at a given moment in the interaction with the patient. This is *not* merely equivalent to what the patient is *feeling*, but rather, what is unconscious yet present, invariant, ineffable, and therefore ultimate reality or "O". Psychic reality in this sense can mainly be accessed through the tools of attention and intuition. For in-depth discussions on the role of intuition and attention, as well as the concept of truth in psychoanalysis, see Bergstein (2022), and Levine (2022).

4 See Bion's (1958) description in *On Arrogance* of the trifecta *stupidity*, *curiosity*, and *arrogance*, in the psychological catastrophe of the failed intercourse with emotional reality.

5 Of course much has been written on this idea. See Souter, 2009; Brown, 2012; Likierman, 2012; Ehrlich, 2017.

6 We may *imagine* this. Of course, we don't know from the record if Bion ever did read this poem, though it was widely read at the time of the war. The poppies themselves

are the clue, but not the invariance, the latter being the emotional experience of their *poppiness*.

7 I would venture to say that if the previously quoted excerpt with his "driver Allen" in the shell-hole in Flanders Field is another re-telling, at this point it is no longer a narration but an evacuation-hallucination.

8 Sweeting, whose real name was George Kitching, was born in September 1898, and was almost 20 at the time of his death, exactly one year younger than Bion who would turn 21 a month later.

9 "For though the Soul should die, the Body lives for ever" (Bion, 1977b, p. 38).

10 Leslie Ernest Asser, 1898–August 10, 1918. Tank Corp, 5th Battalion.

11 There is a mystery here. If Bion is correct that the other runner was Sweeting's (George Kitching) brother, than this brother could be none other than Arthur Cyril Kitching, Sweeting-Kitching's 17-year-old brother. We know that the age of conscription in England during the first world war was 18, but other sources indicate that boys as young as 17 were able to convince recruiters to turn a blind eye to allow them to join. See Peter Jackson's documentary, "They Shall Never Grow Old", for more information on this. But there are two contradictions in Bion's accounts, and perhaps one other: In *War Memoirs*, Bion writes that the other runner brought Sweeting to the medical station, which would mean this was Sweeting-Kitching's younger brother Arthur. In *The Long Weekend*, it is Bion himself who brings Sweeting-Kitching to the infantry who then deliver him to the medical station, and the other runner "disappears completely" in the fog of war, which Angeloch (2021) takes as a sign that he was fatally hit, a conclusion Bion's reader can also draw. That is the second contradiction. The third contradiction is the fact that Arthur Cyril Kitching did not die in the First World War, and although there is no known record of his death, his military record shows that he served in the British Army from 1917–1919, a year after Bion and Angeloch would have had him "disappear completely". These facts can be easily researched by searching the online records of the Commonwealth War Graves Commission and cross-referencing with FamilySearch.org. In my reading, they not only relate to the "facts" but to "emotional truth" and are not as much contradictions but evidence of a T(+H) of Bion's experience. We have to wonder, as I do later in this chapter, if it is not Sweeting's "younger brother" but Bion's—his close friend Asser who in fact did not survive the war—that Bion's memory transforms through a hallucinosis of guilt.

12 In Bion's narrative, this is True if we consider this narration of his trauma as the aesthetic attempt of Knowing what occurred to him that day, August 8, 1918, when both he and Sweeting "died". The historical record indicates that Sweeting-Kitching died the following day, on August 9, 1918. As in my previous footnote relating to Sweeting-Kitching's younger brother, the facts of their deaths or survival are not just that but may be seen as T(+H) of Bion's emotional truth and psychical reality. Bion has something to say about this in his preface to *The Long Weekend*, where he writes, "In this book my intention has been to be truthful. Without attempting any definition of terms I leave it to be understood that by 'truth' I mean 'aesthetic' truth and 'psychoanalytic' truth; this I consider to be a 'grade' of scientific truth. In other terms, I hope to achieve, in part and as a whole, the formulation of phenomenon as close as possible to the noumena" (1982, p. 9).

13 This is in line with Grotstein's observation that alpha-function includes both the primary and secondary processes, in dialectical relation to each other, and existing in the registers of both the unconscious and the conscious (Grotstein, 2007, pp. 80, 321–322).

14 I'm omitting here Bion's memoir, *All My Sins Remembered*, as this contains only one, very brief references to the First World War. However, this reference is to Asser's death (1985, p. 63).

Chapter 2

Transformations in negative and positive hallucinosis

As I stated in the introduction of this book, Bion's use of his concept transformation in hallucinosis, T(H), is often obscure in his texts. After reading through both *Transformations* and *Attention and Interpretation*, it is easy to agree with the authors of the entry to "transformations" in the *IPA Inter-Regional Encyclopedia of Psychoanalysis* that "the relevant texts" on the subject "are unclear, vaguely mystical, and often quite ambiguous" (IPA p. 705). As an example, we can compare two passages from Bion. In the first, written in 1970 in *Attention and Interpretation*, Bion writes:

> In the domain of hallucinosis the mental event is transformed into a sense impression and sense impressions in this domain do not have meaning; they provide pleasure or pain. In this way the unsense-able mental phenomenon is transformed into a beta-element which can be evacuated and reintroduced so that the act yields not a meaning but pleasure or pain.
>
> (p. 251)

Bion here is explicitly describing a process involving visual hallucinations.[1] These are positive hallucinations in the sense that something appears in the visual field with no referent to an actual object behind it. In fact, in a footnote on the same page, Bion makes the interesting observation that hallucinosis grants a degree of independence from the object. The "mental event", that is the experience as it exists in the mind, is de-codified from anything bearing meaning back into a sense impression, a beta-element limited to producing pleasure or pain in the subject and in this way loses its referent. We can think of this as a movement *in the negative*, that is from greater connection between sense impressions and meaning, to lesser or weaker connection between now regurgitated and expelled sense impressions and the psychological content they initially generated. A movement occurs, then, from K→O (IPA, p. 705). Devoid of meaning, the subject is in a state of experience. With considerable work from the analyst, the fragments of visual images projected into limitless space can be dreamed into reassembly through the analyst's use of reverie and his representational imperative (Levine, 2022). This process of decodification and evacuation is famously described by Meltzer (1986), who writes of the

DOI: 10.4324/9781003520740-3

frustrated child who breaks the Lego figure. The figure's scattered remains, some of which are still stuck together, show evidence of having previously meant something. Now in pieces, they are not constantly conjoined in any manner that would reveal the figure that had once been. But Meltzer's formulation of Bion here is interesting because it is the first in the literature to get close to the distinction I am bringing out between negative and positive hallucinosis. He explains the difference that Bion makes between hallucination proper and transformations in hallucinosis in terms that seem to relate hallucination to its *positive* form, and transformations in hallucinations to its *negative* form akin to an experience denuded of meaning. Here is Meltzer (with Scolmati) in his own words:

> The transformations in hallucinosis are different from hallucinations in that they do not involve the perception of objects that are not there in external reality, but they involve the perception of relationships that are not there. That is hallucination involves the sensory experience of bizarre objects, and these are bizarre for the reason that they exist outside the system of meaning—they are meaningless objects and therefore they belong to the general world of delusions and delusional systems. But although transformations in hallucinosis are within the world of symbol formation, thought and meaning, there is something disordered about the quality of thought that has gone into them. And this produces something similar to poverty of imagination and rigidity.
>
> (Meltzer & Scolmati, 2009, p. 107)

Now, Meltzer gives a case example following this description that seems to describe processes with his patient that involved, among many details, the reporting of misperceptions of the analyst (that Meltzer looked as if he were sick with heart disease; misunderstandings taken as fact; being accused by Meltzer of being a racist) and dreams that function as hallucinations of the analytic interactions. Meltzer does not parse out for the reader how he categorizes each of these clinical phenomena. However, located in a chapter entitled "Transformations in Hallucinosis", and in the light of the above description, I read his descriptions to be of the co-existence of positive hallucinations, T(+H), in various examples visual, tactile, olfactory, with a concrete experience of reality, T(−H). That is, the patient's experience from their unconscious point of view, framed by selected facts consisting of projected, mutilated alpha-elements, constitutes the whole of their conscious point of view. Here, the caesura between the two registers of the conscious and the unconscious is overly-porous when not collapsed. This is what Meltzer means when he defines hallucinations (positive hallucinosis) as those which involve the perception of *objects* that are not there, and transformations in hallucinosis as involving the perception of *relationships* that are not there. Both processes involve the projection of the "Lego pieces", in an operation where "something that was about to be constructed in his mind is destroyed and the debris from this reversal of alpha-function is evacuated in one way or another" (Meltzer & Scolmati, 2009, p. 113).

The "poverty of thought" and "rigidity" that Meltzer describes in what he refers to generally as T(H) refers to the absences of thinking and emotional linking of elements in an experience that would bring it to life in a way that represented a true co-construction between lived internal experiences and external impressions. In fact, "poverty of imagination" and "rigidity" indicate a disinvestment of the external field of perception in favor of a withdrawal into the internal realm, with a consequent flooding of the external space with projected mutilated alpha-elements. Post-projection, meaning is no more arrived at or thought about as it is "given" through the reintrojection of the remaining stuck-together Lego pieces taken now as thing-in-themselves. These now unrelated pieces are taken to form new relationships, essentially "the perception of relationships (between the Lego pieces) that are not there", the way that in a cubist painting, an eye here, and a tooth there can create a form much more menacing than a more symmetrical rendering of face. A bizarre object is formed by the misperception of the relationships between its parts; however, the connection with the de-cathected reality is preserved even while scrambled, so that a conviction of truth behind the delusion remains. A space where meaning ought to have been created has collapsed through de-cathexis, leaving behind a void onto which delusional object relations are now projected, as "attempts to patch over the internal absence" (Reed & Baudry, 2005, p. 138), which remains inside the subject as a *fact* causing him pain. As Bion reminds us,

> one of the revolutionary and disturbing theories in psychoanalysis is that it is questionable whether anything is forgotten in the sense of really disappearing. The important point about Melanie Klein's idea that at a very early stage the infant has a phantasy that it is able to split off what it does not like and evacuate it, is that it is an omnipotent *phantasy*; nothing happens, the situation remains unchanged, the personality remains unchanged. However, there is now an added layer of this phantastic belief that something has been gotten rid of. But suppose that it is not forgotten, that it simply becomes part and parcel of an archaic mentality, unconsciously thought—in spite of the contradiction in terms—which is extremely active.
>
> (1976–1979, p. 130)

So now the individual has *two* problems: the void and the T(H) that attempts to patch it up. In the example of Bion's poplar trees hallucination from the previous chapter, Bion negatively hallucinated the path he took, and in its place, he positively hallucinated the path taken by his guilt-ridden superego. The relationship between the tall blades of grass shooting upward, to themselves and not to the poplar trees could not be seen, or rather, were unseen, negatively hallucinated. In its place stood a road of hallucinated poplar trees leading in the direction of his sense of incompetence and guilt, which did not dissipate.

Another example of this is from a patient who I will discuss in Chapter 4 (Mr. D), who believed that the helicopter circling overhead was stalking him. The patient negatively hallucinated, that is, made invisible and could not see, the links between *this* helicopter, *a* news helicopter, the city apartment he lives in, and the metropolitan city where his apartment is located to assemble the "common-sense" (Bion, 1958–1979, p. 17) reality that there was always a helicopter hovering over the city where his apartment was located that had nothing to do with him. We can see that these beliefs constitute another form of Meltzer's "perceptions of relationships that are not there" or put in other words, negative hallucinations of the relationships that *are* there. These relationships are what the patient still cannot see when they are pointed out to him. The patient fills in the vacuum with pieces of the destroyed intolerable inner reality of his cruel and persecutory superego and transforms the helicopter into a bizarre object, a positive hallucination, created by the negative hallucination (disappearance) of its connections to reality. Why is it *bizarre*? Because for the analyst, the helicopter does not need any explanation, but for the patient, its appearance is bizarre. "Isn't it *strange*", Mr. D said, "that the helicopter is there *again*?" For the analyst, the helicopter overhead is both a thing-in-itself (its meaning of being a regular news helicopter is obvious and does not have to be interpreted) and in relation to his patient a conventional symbol (Calamandrei, 2022, p. 769) of the patient's unconscious (or unformulated) sense of guilt and self-hatred. For the patient, the helicopter is a non-conventional symbol (ibidem) and in that way, *only* a thing-in-itself realizing (making real) the patient's guilt and self-hatred bearing down on him. There is no other possible understanding or experience of the situation for him. The situation is one of "poverty of imagination" and "rigidity" as no exploration can be made of an experience that, having been transformed into total suspicion, cannot be doubted. But the void that the helicopter hallucinosis (+/−) attempts to cover up remains in circulation as it lies at the juncture of where the subject's thought processes meet and fail to withstand the emotional impact of his experience in given situations, be they of separation, transition, or other of life's challenges where coming into being is what is in question. Every attempt to evade the pain of frustration widens the void if it reinforces de-cathexis as a solution, throwing out of use the ego's healthier ways of linking with reality.

The idea of negative hallucinosis leads us to questions in psychoanalysis, and in Bion's work, on how we theorize negative space. To think more deeply about this, let us look at a second passage where Bion discusses T(H), in what is the second time he writes about it in his oeuvre, here in *Transformations* (1965):

> If there is a "no-thing" the "thing" must exist. By analogy, if Falstaff is a no-thing Falstaff also exists: if it can be said that Falstaff, Shakespeare's character who had no real existence, has more "reality" than people who existed in fact, it is because an actual Falstaff exists: the invariant under psychoanalysis is the ratio of no-thing to thing. But +. And −. can coincide; in this case the patient who displays a state of mind approximating to this representation regards the analyst who is actually present as also the *place* where the analyst is not. Conversely, the analyst who is actually absent is regarded as a space which is occupied by the absent analyst.
>
> (p. 218)

Bion footnotes this last sentence by referring the reader to an earlier chapter where he mentions T(H) for the first time in his writing, but there it appears merely in passing, noting it as an alternative to verbal transformations but then dropping the topic altogether to continue to develop his general ideas about transformations (1965, pp. 187–188). Earlier in the page he adds, "the rule that a thing cannot both be and not be is inadequate" (ibidem). I think Bion footnotes this reference to T(H) in order to begin to link the relationship between the thing and the no-thing with the collapse into the *nothing*, first postulated in *A Theory of Thinking* (1962a). My sense is that Bion here is pushing his thinking further into contemplating processes of de-hallucination, or of negative hallucination of the no-thing, an abstraction of space that will not hold, that devolves into a subtraction of space. If the no-thing is the *place* that holds the thing in its absence, and in turn that space cannot hold because the pressure of the absence (or excess of over-presence) is too much, this pressure is lessened through further abstraction, until there is no center, no point (Civitarese & Berrini, 2022b), and only *nothing* exists, the subtraction, a hole that cannot hold anything.

The description in Bion's previous quote of the "place where the analyst is not" and "a space which is occupied by the absent analyst" bears a strong resemblance to André Green's depiction of negative hallucination:

> The maternal object, in the form of the primary object of fusion, fades away, making way for the ego's own cathexis which are the source of his personal narcissism. Henceforth the ego will be able to cathect its own objects distinct from the primitive object. But this effacing of the mother does not make the primitive object disappear completely. The primary object becomes a "framing-structure" for the ego, sheltering the negative hallucination of the mother.
>
> (Green, 2001, p. 193)

This "framing-structure" relates to Bion's notion of a preconception for the realization of the breast giving birth to thinking. The "framing structure" is the no-thing. Under the wrong circumstances, however, the absent object, rather than stimulating thinking and generating the no-thing that holds thoughts, instead gives rise to the *nothing*. In this way, when negative hallucination leads to the creation of the no-thing, it is under the sway of the life drives. It creates space by letting go of the object and allowing it to become an abstraction. Conversely, negative hallucination is under the aegis of the death drive when under pressure it goes farther and gives way to nothing (see Perelberg, 2015, p. 184). *Nothing* is the first negative hallucination of thought (Green, 1986; see Perelberg, 2017, p. 68), a morbid process that takes the negativizing of structure to further lengths, ensuring that the tantalizing breast is divested not only of meaning, but of the space onto which future meaning, realized through the object, or Falstaff in the earlier quote, may begin to exist.[2] For me, this is the domain of T(−H). Bion helps us speculate on its functions when he writes, "Hallucination (and we can include both types) is seen as a method of achieving independence which the patient considers to be superior to psychoanalysis" (1965, p. 245; parenthesis added), the latter seen as involving dependence on an analyst that for various reasons may be experienced as too frustrating to tolerate.

In *Transformations* (1965, p. 245), Bion lists several observations on hallucinosis, among them that "the concept of hallucinosis needs to be widened to fit a number of configurations which are at present not recognized as being the same", as well as the conclusion that there is a hallucinatory element to transference and projective identification. Following his thinking, in transference (referred to as rigid motion transformation by Bion), the real analyst has to be *unseen*, in a sense negativized, in order to provide a space into which the analyst of unconscious phantasy can become positivized in hallucination. It is later, in *Attention and Interpretation*, that hallucinosis begins to refer to the evacuative debris most commonly associated with it, but also to the observational and listening stance that the analyst must assume vis-à-vis the patient's emotional reality. Developed between the writing of *Transformations* and *Attention and Interpretation*, this observational stance for Bion is one devoid or negativized of memory, desire, and understanding. Thus, this well-known passage from *Attention and Interpretation*:

> Receptiveness achieved by denudation of memory and desire (which is essential to the operation of "acts of faith") is essential to the operation of psychoanalysis and other scientific proceedings. It is essential for experiencing hallucination or the state of hallucinosis. This state I do not regard an exaggeration of a pathological or even natural condition: I consider it rather to be a state always present, but overlaid by other phenomena which screen it . . . to appreciate hallucination the analyst must participate in the state of hallucinosis.
>
> (1970, p. 250)

I take this statement to mean that Bion thinks of hallucination and T(H) as states where alternate positivizing and negativizing processes coincide, underlying and undergirding the thinking process itself, and in which the primary processes of the unconscious ego are awash. The analyst's technical stance as indicated here by Bion is one where he should both experience (positive) hallucination, i.e., see or experience something that would add or create meaning, as well as achieve this through a state deprived of sensorial support, itself reached through the denudation of the analyst's common referents of meaning. These referents, known as memory, desire, and understanding, are the cognitive structures the analyst has built into his network of representations vis-à-vis the patient and are what the analyst has used *to think* the patient. Now Bion asks the analyst to negatively hallucinate or transform into negative hallucinosis the patient and the analytic experience to approximate as much as possible the O of the encounter, in order to stimulate the positive hallucination of new thought, borne of O, or put another way, to stimulate transformations in O. It is possible that some of the confusion around T(H) in our literature has to do with this double meaning of the term, as pathological symptom *and* desirable technical stance. This confusion deepens when we do not specify between positive and negative transformations in hallucinosis in the first place.

We will see later in this chapter and throughout the book how T(H) has come to cover a variety of phenomena. Varied as they are, I contend, the differences are important. If in the literature we can find abundant samples of T(H), the same may not be said of T(−H), although some do exist, including in the important and controversial debate between Sandler and Civitarese in the *International Journal of Psychoanalysis* in 2015. There, Civitarese dedicates some discussion of T(−H), without referring to it in these terms, and even connects it to André Green's negative hallucination. But in general, T(−H) does not appear in most discussions and case presentations in our literature as opposed to the more common attention given to T(+H). This may be due, in fact, to the undertheorization of T(−H), an absence, if the reader will forgive the pun, that this present book is meant to correct. In my experience, T(−H) regularly play a role in the difficulties encountered in the work with non-neurotic patients and when not apprehended, can deteriorate the symbolic functioning of the analytic pair and lead to impasse and the breakdown of the treatment.

I would like to introduce here an experience, one of many, that inspired me to clarify how I view T(−H).

That is just what I said to you!

Ms. S was growing frustrated with what she felt was my inability to say something that could help her think about her experience. Increasingly, she felt that what I told her was merely a concrete reflection of what she had just said to me. I, on the other hand, felt that Ms. S spoke in disjointed fragments with very thin content that gave me too little to think about, and I did my best to string together and articulate emotions and thoughts into coherent forms. When possible, I tried to add something of my own. Wild thoughts, memories that came to my mind while she was speaking, sudden flashes of insight about what Ms. S was laboring to convey—all of these were scarce, though when they were present, I seized every opportunity to put them into words.

Ms. S's mode of communicating was to intersperse long periods of silence where she looked away, deep into what seemed to me like states of inner confusion. From these states she would emerge with a few abstract bits of sentences. I sensed that these bits, perhaps clusters of Lego pieces, pointed in the direction of something indistinct, but mostly seemed to signal a state of constant disintegration. That was the visual that vaguely formed in my mind, though I was at a loss as to how to speak to Ms. S about it. In the moments when I did feel I had something I could say, I experienced a sense of being put *through the looking glass*—brought to the world that Alice returns to in Lewis Carol's sequel to *Alice in Wonderland*—where what I had just put together was somehow turned inside out and back into the thing it was in the beginning. "That is just what I said to you", complained Ms. S, "why are you repeating it back to me? Are you trying to make me crazy?"

It would seem here that this type of response from her was produced by her feeling she was being forced to re-introject something that, as it came out of my mouth, was either not alphabetized sufficiently, or, I grew to think, was neutral-ized in such a way that it became indistinct from my patient's unthinkable internal reality. The caesura between Ms. S and me was tenuous, permeable almost to the point of non-existence, allowing for the threat of one Reality to unfold in the space between us and enclosing us within the thing-in-itself.

Ms. S had come to see me six months prior because she felt she could not form thoughts long enough in her mind to hold together as ideas. She felt she often did not "know" what she was "thinking about" in many ordinary situations. She was highly functional in some respects, and part of her urgency in seeking help was her concern about not being able to function in her new position after a promotion. Still, Ms. S had reason to suspect she suffered from schizophrenia, and often felt that the inside of her mind was disintegrating or "catching fire". Her meetings with her supervisor felt to her frustratingly identical to her meetings with me, where nothing he nor I said found any harbor inside her mind. Transference interpreta-tions were considered moot—"Yes", she would reply, "both you and he (and her father) do the same thing to me. And that is what I just told you!" Ms. S was on a cocktail of anti-psychotic medications, but my impression was that somehow she had managed to neutralize the effects of these too.

Although I had been working with Ms. S for almost one year, twice weekly, every session felt to me like it would be the last, anxiously sensing that what Ms. S left with was not nearly enough to help her feel she had something to return for. *Through the looking glass*, Ms. S herself often said that every session felt to her like *the first* and that we were always starting over. Hearing this repeatedly made me think that she was inhabiting a world entirely devoid of memory, desire, and understanding, a world of O, but completely taken in by it, without recourse to mul-tiple points of view in the way Bion described *binocular vision* (1965, p. 185). My knowledge of the fate suffered by Ms. S's previous therapists when they inevitably lost control of their emotions—one in an intense analysis of several years—hung over my head like Damocles' Sword. The pressure this threat wielded on me inter-nally tested my own recourse to binocular vision, as I felt enormous pressure to *think* where simultaneously there was *nothing* to think about in both my and my patient's minds.

Over time a situation began to develop where I could no longer find anything I said to be meaningful. Anticipating Ms. S's frustration, anger, and the disorgan-ized state that this would leave her in, I began over-thinking what I thought of shar-ing with her, attempting as much as possible to understand *why* I wanted to say it, but then hearing it as if from Ms. S's point of view. Through this filter my words became meaningless. Although different, the additional slant, the depth or changed perspective I felt I was adding no longer felt salient, and I too began to feel I was merely repeating what my patient said, albeit in a form so different that it was the same in disguise. Additionally, Ms. S silenced me when I tried encouraging her to explore her feelings, demanding that *I* tell *her* what *I* really felt. When I did tell her what I felt—for example, at a point when she was complaining about the effort she spent on making it to a worthless session after waiting all weekend, I said, "I think you need to feel I have nothing of value in order to feel that you don't rely on me when you are not here"—she responded concretely as if to a concretely stated statement. In this example, she responded that if I *did* have something of value, I should share it with her, instead of again repeating back what she had just said. We can see here that I was *not* repeating back what the patient said, but rather my words, and what they were meant to add in meaning to the patient's initial communication, were transformed in her mind, and later in my mind, into what she had just said, leaving me to feel I indeed had nothing of value to think or say. The space between the present (what I now think I meant and said) and the past (what I initially meant and said) collapsed, as my new alpha-element (the interpretation) was de-codified into Ms. S's beta-element (the experience of meaninglessness). Not perceiving this, and under the pressure of anxiety, I began predicting Ms. S's dismembering responses to the effect that I could also "see" the meaningless in all my words, the substantive connective tissue uniting them dissolved. To my mind, this is the process Meltzer describes earlier in his depiction of what I felt to be T(−H), where the relation between objects/words is altered to project an alternate reality that reflects the unidimensional pole of the patient's non-represented internal state. Because all words led to the same anxiety-provoking responses, all words were the same, and everything said between the two of us became reduced to different variations of the exchange "you don't understand me" "you feel I don't understand you". Sooner or later, I began having difficulty thinking any thoughts at all. My psychoanalytic functioning had devolved into an evacuative, dismantling functioning, where my own ideas were transformed into beta-elements and in this way negativized. By this I mean I *stopped* having thoughts.

On another channel (Cassorla, 2008), however, I began to think of my experiences with Ms. S as products of a reversal of alpha-function in my mind and in the analytic field.[3] This process of reversal of the directionality of meaning, to the point that it morphs into the superimposition of non-meaning onto meaning, is one that takes place in what Bion called a *reversal of perspective* where two distinct realities are taken to be one and the same. The two observers see one figure in the foreground, the vase, and deny the existence of the two faces in the background. In Bion's example of reversible perspective, taken from *Elements of Psychoanalysis* (1963, p. 48), the patient denies the reality and subsequent effect of his interpretation by accepting the interpretation but substituting the assumption undergirding it with the patient's own assumption, thus converting it in his mind into the same thought. Ms. S may not have accepted my interpretation but took it in as if the assumptions undergirding it were her own, which she then projected onto me, and I took in as my own, transforming the patient's internal reality into a shared external reality.

After a process of internal working through I was able to step outside of myself to catch a glimpse of what was happening in the psychoanalytic field between Ms. S and I. Slowly, I began to understand that my by now internalized process of disassembling my own psychological productions was similar to Ms. S's breaking apart my words, and of her own thoughts. Just as the analyst aims to inject the patient with his implicit alpha-functioning (Cassorla, 2008), so too can this process be reversed, and when working with non-neurotic structures there is a danger that either party injects in the other their own implicit anti-alpha-functioning. Because I was able to hold on to my capacity to discriminate between our two experiences, as Cassorla suggests behooves the analyst working in these states of "non-dreams-for two" (ibidem, p. 161), I was able to grasp that Ms. S was in an important way communicating to me her style of managing terrifying feelings of separation, need, and helplessness. In effect, she was teaching me through experience how to dismantle my own connections between myself and my mind, and between the two of us, until there was little remaining to justify occupying the same space together.[4] The dissolution of the links between her mind and her objects—including her own thoughts—produced the disintegration feeling that terrorized her from the inside, and in relation I was now getting a taste of what it felt like to lose my mind. Projecting these proto-emotions into me, and in turn animating the experience from which my interpretations emerged, Ms. S *realized* the terrorizing disintegration as if coming from outside of her. Now symmetrical, both inside and outside disintegration fused into the one Reality of disintegration.

Having undergone this in varying degrees with Ms. S for several months, what eventually helped me retrieve a more effective analytic footing was the experience of letting Ms. S know of an upcoming break in our schedule. Ms. S responded in a sad tone, saying she was disappointed, as having sessions gave her day a sense of direction and purpose. She was worried about being alone with her thoughts in lieu of our appointment. She then withdrew into silence where she seemed internally preoccupied for several minutes before she emerged and with renewed gusto said,

I don't even know why I keep coming here. These sessions don't do anything for me. I rack my brain trying to think what I get out of coming here, but I can't think of anything that sticks and it just makes me feel angrier that I leave here with nothing but feeling confused.

My thoughts had already begun to drift during the several minutes that passed between her expression of sadness and the burst of anger and frustration that followed. However, Ms. S's words now began to come together in my mind as a rejoinder to her expressed sadness and constituted a *selected fact* (Bion, 1962b) and a new vertex from which I was able to perceive the latent formulation in her manifest statements as *constantly conjoined* (Bion, 1962a, 1958–1979) into a picture that I began to visualize and dream of a little girl in the midst of a tantrum saying to me, "you are not important to me, and I don't need you *because* you are important to me and I need you, in ways that I cannot understand". I tried to formulate this to her as follows:

You were just describing how disappointing it feels to not come here. It's hard to know what you get from coming to see me, but you do seem to know what it feels like to not have the session to come to. It feels confusing, and you feel alone with your thoughts, and you don't want to feel you depend on something you're not sure about. I think you might then have to make what we talk about here including coming here meaningless in your mind, so that it doesn't matter if you are here or not.

Ms. S was silent but nodded. After a few more minutes passed where I felt she had been considering what I had said, she replied that often, immediately upon leaving my office, she deliberately pushed the memory of our conversations out of her mind.

Transformations in negative hallucinosis and its technical implications

In reconstructing this interchange with Ms. S, I felt that my interpretation relied on many factors that when reflected on theoretically, link together several of Bion's most clinically useful concepts with his ideas on T(H). For instance, as I have been building to in my argument, I began to regard the sense of meaninglessness in our joint-discourse, taking place on and off for several months, and in some respects a feature of our work from the start, as an effect of a T(−H). Here, the patient's internal unconscious phantasy of dismantling the links between experience and its significance to her became projectively identified into me, overtime inducing me to begin to carry out similar operations in myself under the pressure of building tension and persecutory anxiety. This affected the way I intervened with Ms. S, which more and more became lifeless and stale. Often my interpretations came from a position of nagging uncertainty, my timing more mechanical and robotic, arising from a place of rote technique rather than *learning from experience* (Bion, 1962b) or contact with the "O" (Bion, 1965) of the session. Ms. S reacted to my words as to beta-elements, which she could not make use of and felt were being pushed back into her. This cycle produced anger in Ms. S, who did not find a container in me as her analyst who, in turn, evacuated experience back into the field between us, ultimately placing her in a position to re-introject more dismantled beta-elements.

After I learned from the experience of Ms. S's reactions to hearing about the upcoming loss of the session and of me, my *understanding*—now K derived from the O of how the patient faced the instability of the object reversed the reversal of my alpha-functioning—I was now able to dream the session with the patient, discerning the unformulated unconscious phantasy of *if I dismantle you, you don't exist and I don't need you*. From this vertex I could begin to view the manifest content of the undreamt enacted dream as reflecting the latent unconscious and unrepresented anxieties of absolute dependency and separation on an unreliable and dangerous object. Coming into contact with this underlying emotional reality of the patient, and how it is interwoven into the analyst's unconscious-conscious emotional reality is the same as coming into contact with the field's unconscious emotional reality, what Bion terms the "O" of the session, the basic unconscious phantasy that becomes the condition for the two participants to be able to be in the room together. In other words, the need to evacuate intolerable elements creates a "negative container, (following Bion, maybe '−C'), a resonator, providing endless amplifying feedback between the members of the group and the leader(s)—resulting in the manic combination of elation and terrible destruction" (Bell, 2022, p. 687; parentheses in the original).

Unpacked, this basic unconscious phantasy—a joint phantasy—could be formulated as

> we can be here together as long as there is nothing linking us together, and therefore we don't need and depend on each other (dismantling of the link); if we need and depend on each other, we cannot be here together, because needing and depending on an unreliable and crazy-making object is dangerous.

The theoretical connection between the "O" of the session and Bion's *group basic assumptions,* in this specific case, one of dependency in this group of two, is clear. Now I would like to call attention to some of the technical implications of being immersed in this state and what the analyst needs to do to reverse the flow of the projections and channel them into a thinking process that can become mutual once it has transformed into an interpretive line derived from the O of the session and the analyst's regained capacity to dream and think. At such moments, the timing of the new (though often repurposed) interpretation plays a crucial role in how it finds resonance within the patient. In my example, generated from O, the interpretation constituted what I will call a *living interpretation*, representing what was occurring there and now and with me (Pichon-Rivière, 1956–1957). It was vocalized in an *act of faith*, and therefore carried an intuition that communicated my receptive and understanding state of mind. What matters here is that in prior moments in the analysis, interpretations of similar content may have unconsciously communicated my defensiveness and anxiety, borne out of technical coherence but nevertheless saturated with memory and desire, unconsciously intended to diminish my anxiety over the patient's frustration. They made sense but had to be made for reasons related to diminishing my and Ms. S's anxiety, which was defensively prioritized over the patient's capacity to metabolize them. As such, they were intended to calm us both rather than soothe us, leading to our inability to feel thus contained. Over time, repeated interactions of this type made real the unreal situation of decoupling from the object by externalizing this interaction. In this way, the emotional meeting of two psyches becomes what I have elsewhere called a *hallucinated field* (Barahona, 2022), where the function of the link between the two participants is to evacuate the ability to symbolize or represent experience, ultimately realigning their understanding of the relationship between them with the symbolic equivalent of the original projector's psyche.

Both analyst and patient are involved in creating this situation of negative hallucinosis. The psychic reality of the unlinking of two minds becomes the *one Reality*. As mentioned earlier, Roosevelt Cassorla's (2008, 2018) work on what he terms *non-dreams-for-two* sheds light on this territory, which he too compares to transformations in hallucinosis (Cassorla, 2018, p. 84). For him, a similar state of chronic, stagnant collusion between the analytic pair often shows itself in a long, drawn-out enactment where

> The analyst runs the risk of being engulfed by the patient's massive projective identifications (*non-dream*), losing his analytic capacity. That is, the analyst may himself have his α-function impaired, targeted by the patient's projectiles. In this fashion, the patient's *non-dream* cannot be transformed into a dream by the analyst, and neither of them dream, or rather, they both *anti-dream*. In situations such as these, both analyst and patient remain indiscriminate, symbiotized, in a common and stagnated area of mental functioning. This is a *non-dream-for-two*.
>
> (Cassorla, 2008, p. 163; italics in the original)

As I noted earlier, this form of transformation in hallucinosis, which here I am delineating as *negative* hallucinosis, is described by Meltzer, using the more general term. Returning to his afore-cited work, Meltzer further states that

> Bion's idea seems to be that the transformations in hallucinosis derive from processes in which the emotional experiences have begun to be transformed into alpha-elements, dreamed and thought about, but that then the process is reversed and the dreams and alpha-elements are cannibalized back to a primitive state, similar to beta-elements, which are then evacuated by reversal of the function of the sense organs and taken back in as new perceptions.
>
> (Meltzer, 1986, p. 107)

If we take Bion's astute observations in *On Arrogance* (1958) and later in *Attacks on Linking* (1958b) that the patient communicates to the analyst via projective identification, we can infer here that Ms. S is in a continuous loop with dreaming and non-dreaming at either end, attempting to make sense out of her impressions of me and the meaning of our interactions, and evacuating whatever fragments of meaning she is able to muster up into me, who she now hears as saying what she has said, and pulling me into a new field now composed by the two of us. The downward spiraling of meaning denudation creates a situation where the links between words and the contexts from which they derive meaning become erased, unseen, invisible and in this way, the hallucination—what appears before the senses—is of a negative, of nothing, unbearable and plain Reality, without nuance, context, depth, and signification. In a case like this where T(−H) have their grip on the pair's experience in the session, the new perceptions, made up of broken and evacuated bits-in-themselves constitute the one Reality that imposes a state where no further meaning can be made because meaning is given directly from the bits-in-themselves. In the earlier example, the unconscious phantasy that my and her words "mean nothing" becomes the reality that both Ms. S and I enact and believe, to both of our despair.

Positive and negative hallucinosis

Hallucinosis, Meltzer goes on to write, is more commonplace and ordinary, a fact that Bion (1970) himself recognized when he described it as a state that can be normal, as well as useful and pathological, "representing a condition, a background, where hallucinations could be prompted in both, i.e., the analyst and the patient" (Lopez-Corvo, 2003, p. 137). In ordinary analytic situations, as in ordinary human interactions, moments of T(−H) constituting psychotic functioning are overlaid or intermixed with non-psychotic functioning, and other parts of the interaction are carried out by healthy processing and the creation of meaning. Depending on many factors (the analyst's state of rest and anxiety, degree of training and experience, the nature of the anxieties coming alive in the hour, the analyst's ability to use his psychoanalytic theories as containers, etc.) the psychotic part of the analyst's mind may be the part that becomes engaged to the exclusion of his non-psychotic part, and through which experience is processed. What is in question here, and also what is crucial, is the analyst's access to his non-psychotic part in the service of re-constituting the container and reversing the process of meaning evacuation.

Both Lopez-Corvo's and Meltzer's aforementioned statements refer to how states of transformations in hallucinosis are in essence a hallucinatory experience, i.e., the patient and analyst are in effect hallucinating. I think this line of thinking where a psychotic process undergirds normal thinking in normal people and relates to the functioning of both their psychotic *and* non-psychotic parts, leads to an understanding of hallucination as a process determined to be psychotic or non-psychotic *per se* not on the basis of the hallucinatory activity itself, but on the ability of the non-psychotic part of the ego to receive it as a communication bearing potential meaning. This is the case regardless of the kinds of hallucination involved, be they T(−H) *or* T(+H), although it is likely the case that T(−H) are harder to detect and come to terms with, as their nature involves a more debilitating and fulsome incapacitation of the alpha-function itself, and in so doing taking on the appearance of total reality. All hallucinations (or states of hallucinosis), whether positive or negative, involve the processes that Meltzer previously describes consisting in an aborted meaning-making operation, where elements are evacuated, and re-internalized in bizarre form, rigidly predetermining meaning. In both types of T(H), the analyst can have sensuous experiences without any background of sensuous reality (Bion, 1967, p. 200; Civitarese, 2021, p. 253). When *positive*, a hallucination forms in the patient's and/or analyst's mind, one that is ego-dystonic to the non-psychotic part and ego-syntonic to the psychotic part of either individual, both baring a "shred of meaning" (Meltzer, 1986, p. 107) that if engaged with by the non-psychotic part of the individual, can be used to reassemble the evacuated experience. In session, when the analyst undergoes a visual experience, he may shrug it away or, alternatively, *positively* transform this sensory experience into something that activates the psychoanalytic function of his mind. In essence, this hallucination carries within it the analyst's (and the patient's) burgeoning alpha-elements of the here-and-now-with-each other in the same process of evacuating these alpha-elements from consciousness. To repeat, the difference between this experience and a frankly psychotic one of passively experiencing positive hallucinations is that in the latter, the psychotic subject is unlinked from his alpha-function. In the former, the individual, let's say the analyst, has the capacity to grasp these shredded alpha-elements and understand them through his intuition, borne out of a previous state of *negative attention*. He is now able to use them to construct meaning out of the interaction.

Examples of these positive types of transformations in hallucinosis abound in the recent literature and include not only visual images such as emotional-sensorial pictograms (Ferro, 2002), affective-pictograms (Rocha Barros, 2000), but can also include parapraxis and slips of the tongue. In the first two, the analyst senses ideas, more visual, somatic, affective than cognitive, and these inform him of something otherwise ineffable about the psychoanalytic interaction. Slips and parapraxis are no longer understood as the escape into consciousness of unconscious repressed thoughts but have more to do with creating meaning, rather than hiding it. In this sense, Civitarese's (2023a, pp. 89–90) example of a supervisee's slip of the pen when writing of a patient's Covid fear of "lockdown/look down" indicates to Civitarese that his supervisee may be experiencing her supervisor as looking down on her, and in this way, the parapraxis-hallucination carries the remnants of what had been an attempt at alphabetizing the emotions in the relationship seeking expression. The question becomes not what is the supervisee *not* saying, but rather, what *is* she saying? [5] From this *change in vertex* (Bion, 1974, pp. 89–90) the analyst trusts and stimulates hallucinosis' ability to point to those elements previously stripped away of their meaning and coherence, allowing the hallucination to function as a communication. The question becomes, does the analyst have the capacity to recognize the mistake as a hallucination, and transform the hallucination *in his mind* as a communication, and therefore put it to constructive use by bringing coherence to the otherwise disorganized and mutilated experience?

Ironically a T(+H) is already evidence that a part of the analytic field is, or at the very least was, moving progressively toward the transformations of affects into alpha-elements, however rudimentary. T(−H), however, reveals a move in the opposite direction. Perhaps more common and more subtle, it is interpreted by the analyst as an impasse, a sign of un-analyzability, the patient's resistance, or the analyst's ineptitude. T(−H) are also a sign of the analyst's inability to transform his own sensuous experiences into meaning, thus surrendering the processes to evacuation and reversal of alpha-functioning. This in turn renders progressively thinner the fabric of multidimensional, human reality, a consequence of the patient's evacuation of emotional experience through abstraction.[6] Being less-detectable, I contend it is more treatment destructive, and if left unnoticed and misunderstood, often leads to breaking off treatment or a negative therapeutic reaction. One insidious form this takes, as depicted earlier in the case of Ms. S, is that the patient's and analyst's reason for being together loses total meaning.

It is not uncommon for an analyst working with difficult patients or otherwise to get into the habit of diminishing, ignoring, or pushing away his sensuous experience, along with the unnoticed reveries they trigger, in order to "focus" on what is happening. Often, under anxiety and through the looking-glass lens of the superego, the analyst rationalizes his sensorial experiences in session as just zoning-out, being tired, or distracted daydreaming. In doing so he fails to integrate these experiences into his mind's efforts to bring to his attention the emotional complexity of the present moment. In sum, and to return to *Alice in Wonderland* as an analogy, when the analyst is able to notice his visual sensual impressions in the session as such, we are talking about the analyst's T(+H). These are emotional pictograms that may be thought of as the lone appearance of the smile of the Cheshire Cat. When the analyst uses the hallucinosis to make meaning, the cat's head rematerializes around the smile, and we get a bigger, deeper picture. When the cat's smile frightens the analyst, and for any other reason he ignores or pushes it away, we are describing a step in the direction of T(−H), the smile again being the only thing that remains, now as a sign of persecution, abstracted from the rest of the cat's head which has disappeared into the background in a reversal of perspective. Unless the analyst is able to wrap his own head around it, the smile becomes a link in a regressive chain of T(−H), leading ultimately to the complete disappearance of the smile, followed by the analyst's own thinking and symbolizing capacity— in effect his own mind, leaving only the background of persecutory anxiety from which the hallucination emerged.

This further step in the morbid trajectory of the negative has recently been described by Civitarese as a form of what Bion referred to as *invisible-visible hallucinations*. However, there are important differences in Civitarese's extension of Bion's intriguing term, which he left to posterity to fill in, and the way I conceptualize its metapsychology. But Civitarese's papers shed crucial light in dealing with what I think amounts to the same clinical phenomenon. In the next chapter, I will delve into his thinking in the hopes that our two perspectives can shed new light on these ideas.

As I further distill the differences between the two forms of transformations in hallucinosis, I hope to get across to the reader that despite their similarities, these two forms warrant different qualifiers. This is so in order to ease the clinician's understanding of what is transpiring at a given moment when psychic reality is being drained of all emotional links, or where the debris of emotional links remain outside of the analyst's awareness but in need of reassembly through the theory and practice of reverie, dreaming, and negative and positive transformations in hallucinosis.

Notes

1 It is important to note that Bion uses the term hallucinosis to refer to the state in which hallucinations occur, in keeping with the British use of the terms (IPA, p. 705). See also Barahona, 2022, p. 88.

2 In Chapter 3, I will delve into the difference between the negative hallucination of the mother, as the creation of the framing structure that holds the future hallucination of the object, with the negative hallucination of thought, the destructive, void producing process

that is the end result of what I am calling transformations in negative hallucinosis. For discussion on these distinctions, see Perelberg & Kohon, 2017.

3 I am using the term *analytic field* purposely here to describe the *gestalt* formed between my patient and I where a reality of non-meaning reigned.

4 *Dismantling* is a form of foreclosing meaning, or in Meltzer's terms *aesthetic impact*, by keeping information from the senses separate (Meltzer & Scolmati, 2009). While not necessarily constituting an attack on the senses, it dissolves the links between them that would construct meaning. As I will describe in the pages to follow, transformations in hallucinosis comprises a similar form of evacuation of the elements used to construct meaning.

5 A shifts of focus of this type marks psychoanalysis' epistemic move, through Bionian field theory, from a hermeneutic of suspicion to a hermeneutic of trust/faith (Civitarese, 2022, p. 108).

6 I will say more about this process in Chapter 3 when discussing Green's (1999b) concept of *negative hallucination* in more detail.

André Green's negative hallucination and its relation to transformations in negative hallucinosis

This chapter is primarily theoretical, in that it attempts to clarify the metapsychology that underpins transformation in negative hallucinosis as I understand it. In order to establish the basis on which to differentiate between positive and negative transformations in hallucinosis, or T(+H) and T(−H), an understanding of André Green's (1999b) concept of *negative hallucination* is crucial. The first part of this chapter will deal with this. The second part will bring into focus Giuseppe Civitarese's work on T(H) and what he has called invisible-visible hallucinations following a few references from Bion. I will delineate how our thinking aligns and diverges on what I think is the same psychical and metapsychological territory that is the subject of this book.

Elaborated over the course of his career, but primarily in his book *The Work of the Negative*, André Green's concept of negative hallucination has been cited often in our literature, but rarely used to the degree and depth that Green himself attributed to it. Green conceived of negative hallucination as a form of what he broadly thought of as the negative and constitutive function of the psychic apparatus responsible for negativing positive elements, leading to the possibility of the unconscious itself, and any other element dynamically related to the systems perception-conscious. Thus, all defense mechanisms, though most emblematically splitting, repression, denial, negation, and projection, involve a negativizing force in the psyche that says "no" to another part and renders it invisible if unconscious or, as in the case of the psychoses, abolished. Here we already see what Green (2005) and others (see Perelberg, 2015) mean when they note that the negative, including in its form of negative hallucination, forms parts of processes that are both constitutive as well as destructive of the psyche, depending on whether they function under the aegis of the life or death drives. This is key, as life drives are formulations allied with binding, objectalization, cathexis, representation, and symbolization. Death drives on the other hand stimulate the opposite processes: unbinding, disobjectalization, suffocation and abolition of representation, dismantling, de-cathexis, and symbolic equation. Thus, when we use the terms *the negative* and *negative hallucination*, we need to be specific as to what we mean.

In terms of negative hallucination, Green postulated two types. The first is *negative hallucination of the mother*, which creates space and provides the framing structure,

DOI: 10.4324/9781003520740-4

a fingerprint of the object mother, or a psychical blank sheet with the impressions of the mother's body still on it onto which to build the hallucination-representation. This internal frame holds space for what through representation will evolve into thoughts. Already here we are talking about alpha-functioning in the earliest form of a pictogramic representation of *the space* the object occupies even in its absence. Put in the language of the drives, the negative hallucination of the mother involves the binding of life and death drives, where the *creation* of negative space that is evidence of the life drives is facilitated by the tempered *de-cathexis* of the object made possible by the death drives. The second type of negative hallucination, the *negative hallucination of thought*, is pathological and destructive in the sense that it dismantles psychic structure and appears when the encounter with the object is traumatic. As a protective measure the ego dismantles its contact with the object (Sekoff, 2022). The unbinding of representation that ensues involves "a pure culture of the death drive" (Freud, 1923, p. 53) and extends beyond the object to the negative space that awaited the return of the object, leaving behind a void into which there is no entry and from which there is no possible return.

Negative hallucination of the mother and the traces of the mother's arms

Green writes,

> The maternal object, in the form of the primary object of fusion, fades away, making way for the ego's own cathexis which are the source of his personal narcissism. Henceforth the ego will be able to cathect its own objects distinct from the primitive object. But this effacing of the mother does not make the primitive object disappear completely. The primary object becomes a "framing-structure" for the ego, sheltering the negative hallucination of the mother.
>
> (2001, p. 193)

For Green, the negative hallucination in general refers to the trace left behind when the psyche disconnects from the object, either because contact with the object is momentarily lost, or is overly traumatic and must be lost. In the former case, where negative hallucination becomes the backdrop onto which representations are to be created, the missing object mother is what is transformed into an internal framing structure in the mind of the infant. This framing structure allows the infant to tolerate waiting for the return of the object and sets the stage for the accompanying reproduction of representations that will result from the re-initiation of the wish-fulfilling hallucination of the mother's breast into that framing structure.

We can see that Green envisions an internal process where, as the ego detaches, the invisible outlines of the object are abstracted from it and left as etchings, a negative print, or substrate, upon which the later mnemic traces (Freud) leading up to the representation of the object will be inscribed via hallucination of the breast. This process allows the ego to reinvest in internal structure building; having abstracted from the maternal object what it needed—a memory of her embrace so to speak—it is freer to cathect other objects, including itself as an object, strengthening and shoring up experiences with its environment and learning from experience—building internal structure. Another way to visualize this process of primordial negative inscription (the negative hallucination) is to imagine the traces left behind in the palm of one's hand once an object is released from its grasp.

However, Green is far from clear on what internal processes are involved in the negative hallucination of the mother at a micro level. He is ultimately unsatisfied with his much-cited original definition of negative hallucination *in general* as consisting of the "representation of the absence of representation" (Green, 1999b) because of how it confuses representation with perception and invokes too many psychoanalytic connotations to the word "absence" not to be confusing (Green, 2005, p. 218). The negative hallucination of the mother is the creation of an absent *space* where the object was and will be, not the ego's representational accounting for its absence. Ultimately it is responsible for the creation of space where contents can exist dynamically in the unconscious in different transformations. From Green's descriptions of what he terms negative narcissism and later, disobjectalization, the creation of this space involves a withdrawal from the object that itself becomes cathected "as a negative capacity at the foundations of the mind, as a processual holding of the mind and its functioning which begins at the dawn of psychical life and has to be reconstituted throughout life" (Delourmel, 2013, p. 139). In a sense, the mind begins to hold space as the object is mourned and released, space that is available for the object's return and as a suture in the case of its disappearance. This releasing of the object—Green uses the word *effacement*, which means to wear away or gradually eliminate—can also be thought of as a process of abstraction of the object. In other words, it is made less and less real, and more and more into an abstraction, which is not the same as an idea. Its outlines, like in the example of the outlines left on the palm of one's hand, are the only signs it was ever there. Green goes on to say:

> Now the effacing of the maternal object that has been transformed into a framing structure comes about when love of the object is sufficiently sure to play this role of container of representative space. The latter is no longer threatened with cracking; it can face waiting and even temporary depression, the child feeling supported by the maternal even when it is not there. The framework, when all is said and done, offers the guarantee of the maternal presence in her absence, and can be filled with fantasy of all kinds.
>
> (2001, p. 193)

Earlier in the same text Green (2001) writes

> Are we not justified in inferring that the negative hallucination of the mother, without in any way representing anything, *has made the conditions of representation possible?*
>
> (p. 86; italics in the original)

If the negative hallucination of the object can then be conceptualized as the mind's process of making something impactful, i.e., the object's painful withdrawal or disappearance, tolerable by way of gradual de-cathexis or abstraction of the object, it is through the child's love of the mother—because its experiences with the mother have been good-enough—that the child is able to hold this empty (negative) space in suspension.[1] The way I read Green, the negative hallucination of the mother is not a representation of anything, but a sustained process of creating empty space in order for the lost object to reappear or be created anew through a positive hallucination leading to representation.

The negative hallucination of thought and transformations in negative hallucinosis

One major problem we encounter when trying to understand what Green meant by the second form of negative hallucination, *negative hallucination of thought or thinking*, and tying it to T(H) in Bion's work is that Green uses the specific term only rarely and describes the processes throughout his work on the negative without specifying it as such or in relation to other forms of the negative. This suggests a significant overlap in the types of negative hallucination Green conceives of. The term itself ends up referring in the main to a form of making an object "disappear" in significance by negativizing the links between its perception and the affect it evokes as well as the representational activity it triggers. The object in question is anything to which the subject is in relation and must respond psychically, from the environmental mother to specific people and interactions with them, including adverse events such as traumatic experiences, and even, as we will see, ideas and psychical functions. Kogan reminds us:

> The "work of the negative" is André Green's (1993) collective designation for mental functions that are designed to reject objects, disinvest perception, and impoverish the ego. Under the broad rubric the "work of the negative," he includes the "negative therapeutic reaction" (Freud, 1923), as well as the mechanisms of repression, negation, splitting, and disavowal. He adds five additional notions of his own: "negative hallucination," "negative hallucination of thought," "subjective disengagement by the ego," "negative narcissism," and the "ego's sense of self-disappearance".
>
> (Kogan, 2015, Fn.2, p. 66)

Disentangling when Green is speaking of negative hallucination of thinking from negative hallucination in general, negative narcissism, disobjectalization, de-cathexis, the processes specific to the dead mother (Green, 2005), and the other situations included in Kogan's footnote is not a feat for the faint of heart. Things are clearer when Green designates separate subtitles for each, but his thinking on these cannot be contained within these limits and perhaps should not be. The flow of his writing reveals to the reader that, for Green, the negative in all of its forms represents one pole of what he sees as an essential oscillation of psychic movements preceding the formation of repression. Green writes:

> When I tackled negative hallucination for the first time, I put forward a model of double reversal . . . on the assumption that a system of functioning exists before repression comes into effect, I assumed that the combination of the turning round upon the self and the reversal into its opposite—the double reversal—created an enclosing circuit, demarcating opposed spaces (internal and external) which could be regarded as a structure providing a frame for psychical space capable of gathering and inscribing representations as well as making them interact.
>
> (Green, 1999b, p. 209; my ellipsis)

Later in the same page he writes:

> What is lacking therefore in the psychoanalytic theory of perception is the need to include it in a space of reversal which we have described for drive investments by including a part linked to the mother's response, for which we have suggested a figuration which helps one to understand the transit external-internal.
>
> (Ibidem)

Two things are important here, the first being that negative hallucination acts on perception more than on representation (Green, 1999b, p. 208). It is a response to an unassimilable perception—that is, it starts at the senses—and triggers from that point on a decoupling of the senses with the representational capacity of the individual. In the first of the previous two quotes this decoupling is subtle, not complete, and initiates the process of creating psychic space for thinking that undergirds all representational activity. The second important thing to note is how Green's double reversal leads to what Reed and Baudry (2005) see as the framework for Green's thinking on the origins of psychic life, aptly described by them in terms of his universe of presences and absences, or positives and negatives. What the double reversal refers to here is the way that negative hallucination works both as creating a template for representability as well as unbinding representations, ensuring the generativity of psychic space.

With the negative hallucination of the mother, described earlier, things are clearer. In Bion's terms, we might think of the negative hallucination of the mother as a form of preconception, awaiting a realization to form a conception that would function as an internalized object mother. The positive wish-fulfilling hallucination catalyzes the traces of the negative hallucination, bringing it back to life in good-enough circumstances. Because this negative hallucination of the mother is generated in the attenuated and good-enough interaction with the primary maternal object, it is said to be *learned from experience* in Bion's sense of the phrase. However, when contact with the object proves too traumatic, either its loss or presence felt in excess of what the subject can tolerate, the process of negativization continues unabated, de-linked from the life drive, until even the trace is gone, producing a tear in the fabric of the psyche. The abstraction of the object that is necessary for thinking reverses into *subtraction*, and the latter takes on a life of its own until only a hole is left, a void where nothing of the original object remains. As Green states, not only has the mother been "buried alive, but her tomb itself has disappeared" (Green, 2005, p. 154). Put another way, the negative hallucination of the mother is negatively hallucinated and disappeared; the pre-conception, an essential piece of "furniture of the unconscious" (Bion, 1958–1979, p. 42) has gone missing in action in the sense that its integrity is no longer verifiable and it is therefore unlocatable. I believe this is in the realm of what Bion was referring to in his *Cogitations* when describing the psychotic's destruction of the means for understanding as opposed to neurotic resistance, where the former is either "a *positive* statement of *inability* to dream or a defiant assertion of a capacity for *not* dreaming" (ibidem, italics in the original). So here we are in the territory of negative hallucination of thought (Green, 1999a, p. 298; 2005, p. 220) or thinking, where the ability to think is what is disabled, and along with that, the ability to form representations of one's affects and experiences.

Negative hallucination of thinking, in its diversity captures the processes involved in the dead mother complex (Green, 1999b). The loss of the object mother being too intolerable, separation from her for whatever reason too long and unbearable, the object is "murdered", but without hatred (Perelberg, 2017). There is no sadistic attack on the mother's representation, but rather a de-cathexis. Here is Green when discussing the effects of the dead mother:

> The category of blankness—negative hallucination, blank psychosis, blank mourning, all connected to what one might call the problem of emptiness, or to the negative, in our clinical practice—is the result of one of the components of primary repression: massive de-cathexis, both radical and temporary, which leaves traces in the unconscious in the form of "psychical holes".
>
> (Green, 1986, p. 146)

Now the dead mother complex refers specifically to a de-cathexis of the maternal object, which creates a hole in the psyche where future encounters with the object will evoke fantasmatic and cognitive activity short of authentic thinking and constitute instead a compulsion to think or imagine, intended to patch up the hole in the form of a patched breast (Perelberg & Kohon, 2017). This activity is what in Bionian terms we would call the projection of a beta-screen. The patient talks incessantly at the object (analyst) as if trying to reach him yet defensively keeps him at bay; or the patient compulsively tells jokes or appeases the analyst as if trying to flood the psychic holes with emotion. All of this is in an effort to maintain some sense of self-organization in the presence of the object. Green likens this situation, where a more or less abolished internal representation encounters an external perception that reactivates it from reality, to a train wreck resulting from two engines catapulting full speed toward each other (Green, 2005, p. 221).

Others apart from Bion have described similar mechanisms as those at play with the negative hallucination of thought, responsible for disturbances in thinking in psychosis and non-neurotic structures. Lacan's *foreclosure* [2] and Freud's *ejection* are the two obvious examples. Quinodoz describes a "hole-object" that the individual creates to defend against psychic suffering and destructiveness against the object and distinguishes it from the "absent object" (Quinodoz, 1996, quoted in Kogan, 2015). As I will describe later, Civitarese's (2023b) and Civitarese's and Berrini's (2022a, 2022b) rehabilitation of Bion's *invisible-visible hallucination* covers the same phenomenon, I think, with some caveats. The term "void" has often been evoked when thinking of negative hallucination run amok, as the word refers to an entirely empty space. However, I think "black hole" captures this phenomenon most precisely because it denotes a void around which something that was destroyed—a star—once existed. It also calls to mind the forces around the black hole which continue to pull matter into it. I think these images adequately represent what Green refers to as the disobjectalization of the ego itself, which entails the disabling of the ability to think as the end result of the total disconnection with the object, the destruction of the space in which it would be represented, and the erasure of the inscribed memory of the process of cathecting and creating an object through representation—objectalization—as a way of negativizing the unbearable experience linked to the object to which the ego has now no relation. Here the ego has reached a state of *negative narcissism* where the impoverishment of its ability to represent experience leads to the loss of its own coherence, consistency, identity, and organization (Green, 2005, p. 222).

Perelberg (2015, p. 184) distinguishes the negative hallucination of thought (which as described earlier does away with the basic framework and hardware through which thought is formed) from the negative hallucination of the mother on the basis that the former is allied with the destructive processes and the death drive while the latter is aligned with the creative processes and the life drive. This is in keeping with my proposal throughout these chapters that T(H) can be of two types that are worth distinguishing as T(−H) farther down on the continuum of an anti-alpha and ultimately subtracting function, and T(+H), bearing the fragments of discarded alpha-elements in an effort at reorganization of the psyche. The difficult, but I think necessary, classification of these two phenomena is no less troubled by the fact that negative hallucinosis, in its function of negativizing the object, constitutes the sine que non prerequisite of thinking, and the base from which thought could build progressively into what Bion calls "no-thing", or the first representation or idea, by aiding in the generation of (potential) space between thing and no-thing. As I have been describing, *in its morbid form* negative hallucination in place of abstracting from the object (leading to ideas, thinking) subtracts from it, stopping at nothing until it reaches a minus, where the compulsion to subtract takes hold of a mind now incapable of sustaining thoughts. To negatively hallucinate moderately leads to the tenuous separation between the object and experience, allowing for a space from which an idea is abstracted to emerge. To negatively hallucinate in extremis leads to the collapse of the would-be space and to subtraction of psychic structure. Green himself links the negative in his work to Bion's -K and attacks on linking:

He (Bion) distinguishes the effects of not-understanding and mis-understanding, an opposition which brings out the essential difference between nothing and no-thing. It will be immediately clear that *mis-understanding* contains an ambiguity which can have certain advantages such as enabling one to have a pleasant surprise at discovering another meaning, just as unexpected and unheard—whereas *not-understanding* puts an end to any process of comprehensive understanding.
(Green, 1999b, p. 8; parenthesis mine, italics in the original)

I will quote again from Green on his agreement with Bion, this time at length. According to Green:

Abstraction is an effect of knowledge. But it would be a mistake to locate it at the end of the process of knowledge, as an outcome of the drives. On the contrary, Bion shows that it is present in the earliest stages of knowledge and relates it to concrete thinking which he does not only see as a primitive state of mind but also as the result of an early contamination of the mind by the dysfunctioning characteristic of the child, or he sees its origins in the mother's dysfunctioning (excessive projective identification, inability to tolerate frustration and evacuation being dominant in the first case, a lack of maternal reverie in the second). This complicity results in an alteration in alpha-function which Bion makes the pivotal point of his theoretical system. He shows this in his seminal paper "Attacks on Linking". -K is not content qualifying the negative in terms of an insufficiency or deficit; it gives it status. Not-understanding is brought into play by the patient's psyche when it is in his interest to stop understanding.
(Green, 1999b, pp. 8–9)

If the reader is in doubt as to what Green means by not-understanding as opposed to simply misunderstanding, or in other words, the radical nature of the de-cathexis of thought he is describing, he continues:

This is a widely encountered phenomenon. It is with psychotic patients, or in Bion's terminology, with the psychotic part of the personality, that the specific nature of this mechanism can be pin-pointed. . . . Certainly, the symbol -K bears witness to the fact that the developmental stages of abstraction appear not to have taken place, but also that psychical activity is aimed at "minus linking". . . . But the devastating consequences of this fundamental intolerance of frustration are linked by Bion to the recognition of the structural attributes of the psyche.
(idem, p. 9)

Green (1999b) refers to this darker side of the negative as the pathological negative "in contrast to the work of the normal negative found in displacement, condensation, and symbolic disguise" (Reed & Baudry, 2005, p. 130). Although Green, to my knowledge, never directly connects the negative hallucination of thought as a term directly with attacks on linking and -K, he does so conceptually under the broad umbrella of the *pathological negative*. Detailing the mechanism involved in the pathological negative, Green writes:

> The analyst witnesses a sort of coup de Jarnac[3] which the patient carries out on his own discourse. It is as if he wants to impede the work of association from developing towards an eventual widening of consciousness which has been strikingly and silently anticipated.
>
> (Green, 1999b, p. 9)

Let us look at this process in more detail.

Attacks on linking and the negative hallucination of thought

According to Green, the primary target of negative hallucination—and here he is staying true to form by referring to negative hallucination *of thought* without saying so specifically—is speech, since he considers language, in accordance with Freud, that which makes thoughts perceptible to the subject (Green, 1999b, p. 207). The subject thus ceases to cathect the object with images that will lead to representations (words), leaving behind instead a concretized carcass that is more easily relinquished. In Bion's terms, the object is de-alphabetized into beta (beta-function) and is evacuated. This is the process of subtraction that is the inverse of abstraction, the latter implying ever higher degrees of thinking about the object. In subtraction, or -K, the cathexis and the burgeoning representations it gives birth to, is withdrawn, the object disobjectalized, and under extreme circumstances, the ability to cathect *itself* is subtracted, the memory of how to do so gone with the object. The form this takes in its most benevolent manifestation is the patient's losing their ability to express themselves in words. I am here using the qualifier "benevolent" lightly, as for Green we are still talking about what Bion would describe as difficulties at the level of thinking, "the non-perception of thoughts through language" (Green, 1999b, p. 196). Blank thoughts, the mind suddenly going blank, the immediate forgetting of something the analyst has just said and was evidently heard, silence that evokes not an absence of words but the absence of the ability to use words as a tool for thinking—these are the phenomenological signs Green alerts us to when dealing with unconscious processes that signal that at a deeper level alpha-functioning is operating in reverse. Howard Levine (2022) has described similar phenomenon when depicting how the unformulated or unrepresented unconscious makes its appearance in the consulting room, through the disorganization of the patient's discourse at certain points, signaling to the analyst specific representational vulnerabilities around certain themes that hit psychic potholes or landmines, to evoke Bion's war experiences, invisibly strewn across the networks of associations. As

Reed and Baudry put it, "On a clinical level, the chain of associative displacements can be interrupted by emptiness" (2005, p. 131). More morbidly, a patient may report that they feel their "brain is on fire", as Ms. S (Chapter 2) often did, "go blank" for the entirety of the session, or present with psychotic delusions and hallucinations with clear symbolic referents viewed from the analyst's vertex, but from which the patient's reflective capacity is drastically severed. This is because while the psychotic part of the patient is overwhelmed by sensual stimuli which the positive hallucinations endeavor to manage and gather in some form (the over-stimulation from the hallucinations is secondary to the unbearable emotional turbulence caused by the incapacity of making meaning out of the circumstances in the patient's life) the non-psychotic part—the part that is speaking to the analyst—is de-linked from its alpha-function and communicates in a way that infuses the consulting room with a deadening haze of concreteness. This is what I refer to as T(−H).

Because alpha-function for Bion can only at first come into operation in relation to another mind, it has a linking function to the object that, in negative hallucination of thinking, is lost. Instead of linking, alpha-function operates in reverse, as a disobjectalizing function. Instead of the presence of an object (formed through objectalization), there is an absence, what we are calling a void or black hole. Absent the link to the object there is no possibility of sustaining meaning or a meaning-making processes, as it is through relation to objects that meaning is created (Reed & Baudry, 2005, p. 130). Reed and Baudry remind us that Green is thinking not only with Bion here in his emphasis on delinking but also with Winnicott, in particular to the latter's revision of his transitional object paper in 1971 where he postulated how the representation of the mother may fade away if the separation, owing to different factors, endures for longer than the child can hold on to the nurturing image (idem, p. 131). They write:

> It is a kind of death, Winnicott writes, but one that leaves a terrifying emptiness, not an image of an object that has been lost. And the return of the mother in external reality does not banish the emptiness. What is there instead of the object representation is a hole in the psyche, a nothing, rather than a no-thing.
>
> (idem, pp. 131–132; italics in the original)

I would like to emphasize here that what I am referring to as T(−H), which involves processes of disinvestment of the representational capacity, is not the passive process that turns of phrases like "leaves a terrifying emptiness" suggest, but an active process of disobjectalization, dismantling, decathecting, splitting, projection, and anything involved in the severing of links between the experience with the object, its perception, the corresponding affect, and the images and meanings that would otherwise flower around these binding processes we refer to as representation. In other words, the negative hallucination of thinking or transformations in negative hallucinosis, entails attacks on linking, which is an active defensive process consisting of the operation of any one of the different defensive maneuvers the psyche has at its disposal that serves to obstruct or destroy the creative process involved in constructing meaning and psychic structure.

Attacks on linking and its relation to objectalization and disobjectalization

In discussing Freud's life and death drives and their relation to binding and unbinding, Green develops the concepts of objectalization and disobjectalization, two functions that are key to how we understand negative hallucination and transformations in negative hallucinosis. For Green, objectalization is the final aim of the life drive, that is, the latter's "essential purpose is to ensure an objectalising function" (Green, 1999b, p. 85). Green is not only clear that he sees this function as surpassing the creation of an object-relation that serves as a link to the object, but also claims that this is where object-relations theory fell short. Putting Freud's (1917, 1923) assertion that the ego itself can become the object of the id into greater light, Green explains how the objectalizing function acts to turn a structure into an object, "even when the object is no longer directly involved" (Green, 1999b, p. 85). But this process is not restricted to structures that are as organized as the ego and can spread to "other modes of psychical activity in such a way that, ultimately, it is the investment itself that is objectalised" (ibidem). In other words, as Reed and Baudry point out, it is not only the object that is cathected, and invested through objectalization, but the investment process itself that is invested in. The function of creating objects becomes itself a capacity that is represented in the psyche (Reed & Baudry, 2005, p. 133). This means that the objectalizing function self-perpetuates the building and integration of psychic structure that defines it, binding, uniting, and facilitating relations between subject and object (ibidem). This has obvious consequences for representation, which would not be possible without at least a rudimentary form of binding.

If this definition of objectalizing is clear in our minds, we can more easily understand disobjectalizing as a function of the death drive to disinvest, decathect, or delink. Reed and Baudry place it squarely within Green's pathological negative, which they also describe as radical destructiveness, even of the objectalizing function itself. This disobjectalizing function as ultimate aim of the death drive surpasses Freud's definition of it, but in an important sense, is also in keeping with his nirvana principle associated with Thanatos. That is, for Green, when unbound disobjectalization moves beyond the de-cathexis of objects and toward the objectalizing function in extremis, a state of negative narcissism obtains, which is an aspiration toward a level zero of psychic tensions. As I mentioned earlier, negative narcissism leads to disintegration of the ego, its boundaries and its abilities to integrate and synthesize experiences into representations, i.e, to symbolize and to think. Green writes:

> The purpose of the death drive is to fulfill as far as is possible a disobjectalising function by means of unbinding. This qualification enables us to understand that

it is not only the object relation which finds itself under attack, but also all its substitutes—the ego, for example and *the fact itself of investment in so far as it has undergone the process of objectalisation.* Most of the time we only observe the concurrent functioning of the activities related to the two groups of drives. But the manifestation characteristic of the destructivity of the death drive is *withdrawal of investment.*

(Green, 1999b, pp. 85–86)

He continues:

In this respect, the destructive manifestations of psychosis are linked much less to projective identification than to what accompanies or succeeds it—the impoverishment of the ego abandoned to a withdrawal of investment.

(idem, p. 86)

For Green, the destruction of the ability to invest in an object is tantamount to the destruction of the ability to think, as investment in an object is what leads to holding it in mind long enough to register the experience and abstract an ideational representation from it. As Reed and Baudry explain, the struggle between the drive functions of objectalization and disobjectalization depend much on the containment function of the mother, which facilitates the binding of the somatic drive manifestations of the infant with memory traces leading to higher levels of representation (Reed & Baudry, 2005). Withdrawal of this investment is executed with the assistance of any number of primary defenses, such as, in the previous example, projective identification, as well as splitting (Civitarese, 2023a), and attacks on linking. I am separating these three defenses advisedly because the three often act in tandem or subsume each other functionally. For example, splitting is performed through the projective identification of one aspect of the object into another created to hold that projection, causing there to be a split between two objects. The inverse is also true where splitting an object allows for the projective identification of some aspects of the object to be separated out from other aspects that can be used to construct another object. Equally, projective identification of intolerable affects can be one way of attacking the analyst's linking capacities and the ego's own ability to link together its self-experience. However, conceptually I think that attacks on linking as an umbrella defense best captures the defensive process that motors negative hallucination and transformations in negative hallucinosis as when viewed through the lens of disobjectalization. At its starting point, what is "attacked" so to speak, what is the target of psychic (dis)attention, is the ability of the subject to link in a rudimentary way with the object, be that a proto object in the form of a sensation that is either obstructed from (trans)forming into a perception that can then be further invested with meaning and finally represented, or a perception whose representations cannot contain the affect they evoke and is dismantled, unbound from its moorings in psychic life and reduced to its base experience of sensation or experience without memory.

Green says as much when he describes that the ultimate effect of the destructive action of disobjectalization is attacks on linking (Green, 1999b, p. 87). With projective identification, which he also sees as part and parcel of splitting, there is at least rudimentary binding and "apparent objectalisation which projection and identification attempt with the projected parts" (ibidem). However, the success of the disobjectalizing function is mostly witnessed through the withdrawal of investment that is manifested in the death of all projective activity, bringing with it the inability to bind sensations into rudimentary forms that could at least delimit the internal from the external. Phenomenologically and experientially this translates into a feeling of psychic death, or negative hallucination of the ego. Where the ego was, there a black hole remains. For experience to collapse into these types of black holes left behind by T(−H) is to denude it of any form of thinkability and instead allow it to settle into a here and now without time or place.

I would like to add here a cautionary note: It is easy to get lost in the weeds on what exactly in the mind is attacked and how, but I think we have multiple models to help us think about what goes into what might be better conceptualized as *forms* of disobjectalization. To my mind, *dismantling*, which is Meltzer's (1975) term for the separation of the senses as an autistic defense against the unbearable conundrum posed by the object on the nascent self,[4] is a form of disobjectalization and attacks on linking as it distances the self from the object and erases the links (negatively hallucinates) between the senses that would give the object psychic presence. What is dismantled is the connection between the senses that would furnish the elements that would make up the object, in other words, what Bion refers to as the "furniture of the unconscious" (Bion, 1958–1979, p. 42) as I mentioned earlier in this chapter. This furniture—alpha-elements—is destroyed by the psychotic part of the mind in order to foreclose understanding and the creation of meaning, as opposed to neurotic resistance where what is attacked (repressed) is meaningful. What the mind finds unbearable at such a primitive level of experience are not thoughts, but *the fact of having to think the thoughts* as preferable and more conducive to survival than discharge into action or psychosis. Thinking links the subject to reality, and Bion reminds us that in all of us there is a fundamental hatred of reality, a reality that enjoins us to learn from experience and to negotiate difficult emotional interactions with others and feel our feelings. In dismantling the furniture of the unconscious, the psyche directs O away from K, away from learning, and into the two channels of action or psychosis.[5] It is the effort away from the binding of elements, be they senses, alpha-elements, or mental functions, and away from thinking, that unite all of these models of primitive defenses and is the function of T(−H).

Giuseppe Civitarese's invisible-visible hallucinations and their relation to negative hallucinosis

Civitarese has recently written on this very same phenomenon I am describing as the destruction of the ability to invest experience with meaning and representation through the disengagement of alpha-functioning facilitated by attacks on linking. At some moment, as I mentioned earlier, a positive hallucination is generated as a projective means of evacuating while still organizing aspects of the subject's experience. In tandem or independently, this evacuation may go as far as expelling the ability to project in the form of a positive hallucination as so much of the ego, including its objectalizing function, has been expelled along the way. What is left is a "void and formless infinite" (Milton). In his interpretation of Bion's *Attacks on Linking* paper, Civitarese rehabilitates a word that Bion used sparingly, and without much elaboration, but that Civitarese sees conceptually implicit in his clinical examples of the patient's thinking processes under assault from the inside: invisible-visible hallucinations (IVH). Bion describes in sparing detail what he means by this intriguing term, which he seems to only use four times in his entire oeuvre, three in *Attacks in Linking* (1958b, pp. 140, 143) and once in *Cogitations* (1958–1979, p. 81). Quite straightforwardly, without much elaboration apart from what can be deduced from the clinical descriptions, he writes that an invisible-visible hallucination is a "visual hallucination of an invisible object" where a

> visual impression is minutely fragmented and ejected at once in particles so minute that they are the invisible components of a continuum. The total procedure has served the purpose of forestalling an experience of feelings of envy for the parental state of mind by the instantaneous expression of envy in a destructive act.
>
> (Bion, 1958b, p. 143)

Bion is describing the destruction through fragmentation of an image that arouses envy, but Civitarese draws a finer point and brings it to the most rudimentary level of representational activity. He writes:

> Rather than thinking that an initial hallucination forms and then explodes, the description urges us more to think of the influx of sensory impressions which the patient is unable to transform, i.e., "dread of imminent annihilation" (1957, p. 266) and which leaves him in "a state that is neither life nor death" (1957, p. 266). IVH then come to resemble more what results from an explosion of proto-sensoriality that sweeps away the first barrier represented by the image, and fragments it *as soon as it forms or has already done so during the process of forming it.* Drones armed with missiles destroy the dream screen of negative hallucination, the "canvas" that normally "supports" the representation, and not so much a representation rendered on the canvas. The image would be invisible in the sense of not yet visible".
>
> (Civitarese, 2023b, pp. 208–209; my italics)

What does Civitarese mean by "destroying the canvas"? We can obviously hear echoes of Green's negative hallucination of the mother/breast as a canvas that is constructed in the psyche onto which budding images, representations, and later meanings will be etched and filled in. As Civitarese alludes to in this quote and later in his text, Green too compares Bertram Lewin's (1946) *dream screen* to the negative hallucination of the breast (Green, 1999b, p. 276). The destruction of the canvas, then, is not the destruction of the representation of the mother but rather of "the mother's tomb" (Green, 2005, p. 154) as I stated earlier when describing Green's negative hallucination of thought and thinking.

Civitarese reminds us that for Bion linking is a psychic activity, an emotional function that cannot be captured in its totality without the ability to think, without abstraction. "There is no emotion or affection that, in so far as it is felt by the subject, is not inevitably touched by what makes self-consciousness possible, that is, by abstract thinking" (Civitarese, 2023b, p. 198). So in attacking the link, the subject not only attacks the object but what connects two objects, be it an interpretation, an oneiric or hallucinatory image, the psychic apparatus as a whole or one of its functions, the ego, thought, the relationship between analyst and patient—in sum, anything that coming together creates a thought (idem, p. 200). "The attack", writes Civitarese, "can simultaneously refer to the intra- or interpsychic domain, and to the activity of representing, or to representation-as-content. In general, the focus is more on function than content" (ibidem). In other words, Civitarese sees Bion's attacks on linking as mostly aimed at the activity of representing, the function of linking, when linking is that which cathects the psychical synapses conjoining verbal thought, the apparatus of consciousness, image (ideogrammatic thought) and emotion (idem, p. 198). "Basically, linking means to abstract, as in symbol formation . . . it happens in language" (idem, p. 201). Civitarese, keeping with his philosophical interests, cites Heidegger on how "only when man speaks, does he think" (1954, p. 16; quoted in Civitarese, 2023b), but interestingly we have seen that Green attributes that same logic to Freud who also felt that language was what made thoughts perceptible (Green, 1999b, p. 207), making it a prime target for negative hallucinations of thought. Without citing him, Civitarese seems to agree with Green that language is always implicated, and he sees this as implicit in Bion: "For images to link beta-elements (raw sensory elements), they need to be "seen" by a human subject. In his own way, between the lines, Bion reiterates the constraint that binds image to language as a social product" (idem, p. 200). Thoughts precede thinking, and both are preceded by language which constrains through human sociality what can be thought about. "Emotional resonances poured into the molds of language" determine semantic and semiotic meaning, which by definition, for human beings is that which is common to several objects (idem, p. 201). Civitarese is sharpening his focus even more here, as he is writing about attacks on linking taking place at the starting point of thought, where sensation meets the beta-element (beta-function) before it evolves into an alpha-element through this very rudimentary function of abstraction, of thinking. It is as if the psychotic part of the mind has assumed the function of Claudio, the psychotic brother of the dysfunctional family in Eliseo Subiela's *Last Images of the Shipwreck*, who every day eliminates a word from his representational repertoire by writing it on his bedroom wall and crossing it out, never to be uttered and therefore thought about again.

The mind has a choice at this starting point, as Bion (1962a) describes in his *Theory of thinking* paper, to either evacuate or to think. Under the circumstances described in invisible-visible hallucinations, as well as in transformations in (positive) hallucinosis, the mind may evacuate by creating bizarre objects, as Civitarese details, in a cycle of expulsion and reconstruction of meaning very similar to Meltzer's (1986) account of the Lego pieces which I described in Chapter 2. However, Civitarese takes this evacuation further, taking seriously Bion's description of the minute splitting occurring across great psychic distances, and here enters the territory of Green's negative hallucination of thinking and what I believe is still functionally another mode of T(H), specifically negative hallucinosis.

When does the strain on the subject lead to such T(−H) or invisible-visible hallucinations? Alluding to Bion's model of container-contained, Civitarese reminds us of how the inability or "unwillingness" of the object/analyst "to take charge of the child's anguish" leads to "the hyperbolic growth of the anguish" (Civitarese, 2023b, p. 203). In the case of Ms. S, which I described in Chapter 2, my inability to take in and dream what she was communicating contributed to my speaking to her in a way that, although in my mind made logical sense, i.e., referred to thoughts I was having about what was happening between the two of us, did not gather enough of her affective experience for her to feel I was truly open to her raw state of existential panic—the feeling that her brain was on fire—and the various derivatives in behavior or speech that emanated from this base experience. My words functioned paradoxically as actions, that is beta-elements, that pushed her experience back into her, hyperbolically amplifying them and leading to more anguish. A cycle of mutual projective identification began taking place where both of our abilities to put words to our emotions that could serve as containers, and not contents, was gradually diminished, and our interactions began to resemble—I might say actually became—a standoff between two hurt, defensive, and misunderstood people who no longer had contact with their inner "representational imperative" (Levine, 2021, p. 801). A transformation in negative hallucinosis was effectuated where the symbolic roles of analyst and patient who dream and think together dissolved into a deadlock between two hurt subjects talking *at* each other, two dangerous and ferocious animals who lose their civilizing capacity (Bion, 1977–1978, pp. 273–274).

In the first chapter of this book, I described Bion's inability to accurately "see" that he was on the correct path during the Battle of Amiens as a T(−H) culminating in and emanating from the experience of nameless dread (ending in O and starting from O). The overwhelmed ego cannot contain the excessive affect but attempts to do so by stripping off layers of its representations, ultimately leading to nothingness and paradoxically, to a form of live psychic death. Civitarese, when describing the invisible-visible hallucination, writes that it is felt as a form of inner implosion, "a dramatic feeling that something has failed without knowing what it is" (Civitarese, 2023b, p. 207), the only thing remaining being "nameless dread", a "minus-object" or a "naughtness" (ibidem), aligning with my earlier description of an extreme form of psychic subtraction. Under "the collapse of psychic space" the patient is "sucked into a void of undifferentiation" (ibidem). Civitarese adds something interesting, noting that if we view this process as static, it offers us a contradictory understanding of invisible-visible hallucination as "an imageless image", which I think corresponds with André Green's first but later repudiated definition of negative hallucination as "the representation of the absence of representation" (1999b, p. 196; 2005, p. 218). If left here, we would be speaking of the negative hallucination of the mother, in as much as there remains a representation/image of a lack of representation/image—in effect an "imageless image". But Civitarese wants us to take a further step where this terrifying image (in other words, the imageless image has become terrifying, uncontainable to the psyche) is made invisible by virtue of it being instantly shattered and evacuated, "as if it had never appeared to the subject" (Civitarese, 2023b, p. 207). I understand this as the image having been retroactively gotten rid of by erasing the very conditions where it could have existed in the first place—the canvas. Not only does one side of the invisible-visible hallucination drip away—the canvas itself, but "the same ability to represent, a kind of 'gluing' the liquid molecules to each other, also 'drips away'" (ibidem). In my reading, this is the same process that Green describes as disobjectalization, which I connected earlier with his view of the pathological negative and specifically to negative hallucination of thought and thinking. Gone with the representation of the space that would hold the positive hallucination that, in its rapprochement with frustrating reality would evolve into symbolic representation, is the ability to represent at all. This function too is disobjectalized, drops away, "the patient's capacity to form visual images is thus impeded" (ibidem). Civitarese writes:

> *IVH involves the simultaneous destruction of both the content and the container, both the canvas and the capacity to paint.* It is like vomiting. You vomit not only food but also the electrolytes that are needed for the proper functioning of the digestive system.
>
> (Civitarese, 2023b, p. 208; italics in the original)

Are invisible-visible hallucinations the same as transformations in negative hallucinosis? Yes.

So far, I am arguing that T(−H) closely aligns with, as it is derived from, Green's negative hallucination of thought, and both are concepts that cover the same clinical and metapsychological ground as Civitarese's invisible-visible hallucinations. However, in Civitarese's texts on invisible-visible hallucinations, there is no mention of a connection with Bion's T(H) as it pertains to negative hallucinations, although he certainly links it with T(H) when it is seen in its positive form, as I mentioned before. A (positive) hallucination is produced, then it is destroyed, followed by the destruction of the capacity to produce further hallucinations from which meaningful representations could emerge. Positive hallucinations have a reparative function for the ego, as Freud already showed with the Schreber case and as Civitarese here reminds us, and at their rudimentary, non-pathological level form the building blocks of representation through their wish-fulfilling function. In their pathological form, positive hallucinations take the form of bizarre objects, that is, objects (people, ideas, inanimate objects, sensations) that are infused with dismembered fragments of unconscious phantasies, proto-images bound to proto-emotions, that function as a defense that aims to "restore shape to experience, albeit at the very limits of consensuality. It symbolically expresses a request and demands a response from the other" (Civitarese, 2023b, p. 209). There is still an other at this stage of the hallucinatory activity, though at the next stage of negative hallucinosis that other disappears, together with the subject's dependent and unstable relation to it. But what Civitarese calls "true hallucinatory activity" is what refers to positive hallucinosis, where "particles of the ego . . . are discharged outside with violence . . . in order to repair the cruel splitting that has occurred in the ego . . . they are glued to concrete objects" (Civitarese, 2023b, p. 210). Invisible-visible hallucinations are the next step, when the ability to objectalize, the minimum of which is contained in the projective activity of hallucinations as Green reminds us, is made to disappear. To reiterate, for Civitarese, true hallucinations, those that form bizarre objects as a means of simultaneously organizing and expelling experience, refer to positive hallucinations, while invisible-visible hallucinations are in a category of their own. I am arguing that instead, they are another form, the negative form, in the category of Bion's T(H).

It seems to me that in his 2015 debate with Sandler on T(H), published in the *International Journal of Psychoanalysis*, Civitarese does describe this extreme form of invisible-visible hallucinations along with the more common positive hallucinations in these terms without dividing them into negative or positive and instead under the general rubric of *transformations in hallucinosis*. In this paper, Civitarese describes in detail the diversity of ways in which Bion used the term transformations in hallucinosis, which he breaks down into basically three forms. First, in the form of a total adherence to concrete reality; second, as physiological hallucinatory activity that infiltrates perception and allows us to know reality by impregnating it with emotional resonance; and third, the analyst's ideal state of mind which correspond to his theories of reverie and the suspension of memory and desire. The first of these three forms, that which has to do with the subject's state of adherence to concrete reality, is comprised of *both* processes I have been previously reviewing, in a cycle of hallucinatory projection into bizarre objects leading to further constriction of psychic space (evacuation=subtraction), leading in turn to greater pressure and hallucinatory projection, all in what Bion termed hyperbole (Bion, 1965; Civitarese, 2015, p. 1095). Fueled by ever more intolerable frustration, this process gradually leads to a state of affairs where emotional experience is restricted to such a degree that experience itself loses its meaning. "We cannot have one without the other." writes Civitarese, "That is what makes *TH*" (Civitarese, 2015, p. 1096). I contend that within this general description of transformations in hallucinosis, it is obvious that there are two destinies for the intolerable material: transformations in *positive* hallucinations and transformations in *negative* hallucinations.

The situation that Civitarese uses as his starting point in describing this hyperbolic cycle is one where the patient is hemorrhaging emotions, creating a void from which he is unable to hold back their subsequent appearance. Because of a traumatic lack of containment, the subject's beta-elements do not find representation. The subject then experiences them in the form of nameless dread, which they defend themselves against by further releasing the emotions into the void. What does this mean, exactly? I think Civitarese, in line with everything I have been describing on Green's work of the negative, is describing a form of unbinding, or disobjectalization, both part and parcel of negative hallucination. He writes, "Connections to emotionally pregnant facts are dispersed across an enormous arc of time and their meaning is diluted almost to the point of dissolution" (idem, p. 1093). In this dispersal, emotion is separated from any of its proto-ideational referents so as to lose any context that would define it. In fact, in this 2015 paper, he is in agreement with Green that this involves negative hallucinations, which there he does equate to "*invisible* hallucinations" or "hallucinations which take away meaning" (ibidem). At this stage, Civitarese is describing a concrete state of mind, with no *real* hallucinations (i.e., positive hallucinations), but rather "a dynamic process which entails an impoverishment of the capacity to be in contact with reality" (idem, p. 1092). He goes on to say that regression can also produce psychotic hallucinations (i.e., positive hallucinations) and that these two processes contribute to a cycle of loss of contact with reality, which as we know for Bion is always inseparable from emotional reality. So in the aforementioned hyperbolic loop, as the subject projects unrepresented beta-elements in an effort to find them "minimal representation" (idem, p. 1094), this same process robs the psyche of an opportunity to develop an emotional container, leading to further projection of frustration and further subtraction of space. Ultimately, the subject makes the object "disappear", and here we must think of radical de-cathexis, the annihilation of the object as Green described in the dead mother and consequently the negative hallucination of thought. We can imagine this as a static dialectic that leads to total loss of contact with emotional reality and the link with the other, in a combination involving a screen of projection followed and preceded by the divestment of emotional resonance with the other such that the subject's perceptions collapse into their sensations and the entire intersubjective experience of living in reality becomes "O", a One Reality of flatness, without categories (Grotstein, 2000). If we note the following use of the terms "hallucination" and "screen", we can see more clearly how closely Civitarese is in his conception of transformation in hallucinosis in this paper to Green's negative hallucination:

> On the clinical level states of hallucinosis and genuine hallucinations create respectively forms of hyper- or neo-reality. Hallucination puts up a protective screen against the potentially traumatic nature of the real; a real which from

the start of life is identified concretely and forever thereafter identified with the object in unconscious fantasy. This screen also functions as a canvas for the pictures which perception pours back onto it. From this point of view the hallucination is a minimal representation. In hallucination, according to César and Sara Botella (2001, p. 44), a process of "primordial abstraction" is achieved which precedes the secondary abstraction of reflective thought. Hallucination and memory are intimately connected. Hallucination is a memory which physiologically acts as a background to perception and thereby safeguards identity. If, however, reality becomes too violent, the hallucinatory screen grows denser, and normal "invisible" hallucination can turn into full-blown hallucination.

(Civitarese, 2015, pp. 1095–1096)

The term hallucination is used in two ways here, where "full-blown hallucination" would mean positive hallucination, and "hallucination" is equivalent to "'invisible' hallucination", and the dialectic is between positive and invisible hallucination. We already saw that Civitarese equates invisible hallucination in 2015 with Green's negative hallucination. So "hallucination" and "invisible hallucination" here refer to Green's negative hallucination of the mother in its structuring function, that which creates the screen or invisible backdrop onto which representations would be "poured in". Civitarese, then, is in line with Green who also thinks (following Freud) that negative hallucination is a prerequisite for thought, the process of abstraction necessary to create the required space for wish-fulfilling hallucination to flourish into representation in the back and forth of holding and containment. Here is Green, succinctly, "Are we not justified in inferring that the negative hallucination of the mother, without in any way representing anything, has made the conditions for representation possible?" (Green, 2001, p. 86). The final step, for Civitarese, Bion, and Green, is when frustration crosses a threshold and the "conditions that make representation possible" are themselves disappeared:

Since the pain is not tolerable, hallucinosis denies the absence of the breast (of satisfaction) and the consequent frustration. The absent breast (zero-breast or no-thing), the pre-conception of which is indispensible for symbolization, is reduced to a "noughtness" and is "hostile, envious and greedy and does not even exist as it is denuded of its existence" (Bion, 1965, p. 134). The void of representation becomes the analytic scene without characters and without emotions. "The emotion is replaced by a no-emotion" (Bion, 1970, pp. 19–20).

(Civitarese, 2015, p. 1097)

Now, "noughtness", "no-thing" are where in 2022a (p. 21) and 2023b Civitarese and Civitarese and Berrini respectively locate the invisible-visible hallucination. "No longer a no-breast (or no-thing), but a nothingness (noughtness) from which they are terrified, a kind of concrete 'hole' that could collapse their residual capacity to represent" (Civitarese & Berrini, 2022a, p. 21).

The authors write that the disappearance of the capacity to symbolize is directly proportional to the increase in anguish and again, we are in the realm of disobjectalization as a mechanism of attacks on linking, the latter the defense these authors have identified as the usual suspect. In all of the above, I am in agreement with Civitarese's descriptions of transformations in hallucinosis and along with his colleague his elevation of invisible-visible hallucinations as an extreme end-product of the process of evacuation of unbearable psychic anguish that may be involved in a hyperbolic loop with positive hallucinations. However, neither of these authors explicitly connect invisible-visible hallucinations as a concept to transformations in hallucinosis. Furthermore, between Civitarese's 2015 paper and the two from 2022 (with Berrini) and 2023b, the link between transformations in hallucinosis and Green's negative hallucination on the one hand, and invisible-visible hallucination on the other, is not mentioned. In the latter paper it is explicitly dropped, despite the fact that, in my careful reading, transformations in hallucinosis in its negative form as described by Civitarese leads to the same psychic void and disabling of symbolization and representational processes as he claims for invisible-visible hallucinations. It is not clear to me why invisible-visible hallucinations might not be better described as the negative form of transformations in hallucinosis that Civitarese already teased out of Bion's work in 2015, and which I am calling here, for the sake of clarity and continuity with Bion, transformations in negative hallucinosis.

When we read Civitarese's comparison of invisible-visible hallucinations with André Green's negative hallucination, we can see the issue more clearly. Civitarese appears to only consider negative hallucination in the form that Green specifies as the negative hallucination of the mother, as "the framing structure" (Civitarese, 2023b, p. 215) left behind in the absence of the object, abstracted to the minimum degree ("a mild or physiological repression", [ibidem]). He states clearly that he is thinking of negative hallucination as the screen onto which positive hallucinations are projected. In contradistinction, he proposes that invisible-visible hallucination is more in line with Winnicott's non-experience of the fear of breakdown (ibidem):

IVH, on the other hand, is like breaking down a painstakingly completed puzzle, destroying the individual pieces and throwing them away. The image (or better yet, the canvas upon which it is depicted) is fragmented, and with it the function of synthesis that corresponds to it. Unlike in negative hallucinations, where the picture cannot be seen because it has been covered with a cloth or because the light has been turned off, in IVH the image is *no longer* there. Either it could not be formed or it has vanished and left only a void.

(ibidem)

To me, it is clear that when the subject in Civitarese's description is "throwing away the puzzle pieces", they are, as mentioned earlier, throwing away "the mother's tomb" in Green's formulation of the dead mother and the pathological negative in the form of the negative hallucination of thinking. So to Civitarese's assertion that "if anything, IVH is the destruction of negative hallucination" (idem,

p. 216), I would only add, "yes—the destruction of the negative hallucination *of the mother*", and in doing so, sets the stage for the negative hallucination of thinking and effectuates completely a *transformation in negative hallucinosis*.

In conclusion, it is the constriction and ultimate destruction of psychic space, through the hyperbolic loop of projection and subtraction of psychic contents and dimensionality, that leads to the final expulsion of whatever there is left of the ego to carry out the functions of symbolization and representation. These states of mind in an individual and in an analysis, when what predominates is the absence of representability and the experience of deadness, concreteness, and psychic anguish in one or both parties, are what I call transformations in negative hallucinosis. This is in line with Bion's general outlines and Civitarese's distillation of the concept in 2015 and follows Green's depiction of the morbid psychological consequences of what he refers to in various places as the negative hallucination of thought and thinking.

Notes

1 Connections here with Marilia Aisenstein's (2020) work, citing Freud (1920) and Rosenberg (1988, 2003) on erotogenic primary masochism as a binding force of countercathexis of the empty space left behind by the denied object are well worth pursuing, though beyond the scope of this book.
2 Lacan postulated that psychosis was predetermined by the foreclosure or unrepresentability of what he termed the signifier of the *Name of the Father*, or *Paternal Signifier*. This designates the cluster of representations, linguistic and otherwise, around the experiences of subjective individuation from the mother, and the presence of the third object, the father, as mediator and instigator of that separation. Given the presence of an original cluster of non-represented experiences around separation from the primary object, future experiences that call forth would-be acquired aptitudes around these types of experience fall into a void of unrepresentability, triggering compensating psychotic defenses.
3 A "coup de Jarnac" refers to a sneak or treacherous attack. The use of the term originated from a duel in 1547 between Guy Chabot, the Baron de Jarnac, and his opponent who he defeated by unexpectedly striking him behind the knee.
4 What Meltzer (1978/2018, 1986/2018) terms the "aesthetic conflict".
5 I am reminded of a story I heard early in my training of a candidate who was feeling pressure from her supervisor to get her patient to use the couch. Unable to think through the patient's resistances, or her and her supervisor's field resistances in supervision, the candidate opted to remove all of the furniture in her consulting room minus her own chair and the couch, giving the patient no other choice but to lay down. Thus, the removal of the actual furniture of the consulting room actualized the internal inability to furnish mental furniture, and in fact evacuated it, as a last-ditch solution to her relational difficulty with both patient and supervisor.

Chapter 4

Clinical implications of transformations in negative hallucinosis

Enactment[1]

In this chapter, I hope to go in-depth into situations where transformations in negative hallucinosis, T(−H), produce exceptional clinical challenges. Considering how ubiquitous and in some ways, silent, T(−H) may often be, it is often an enactment that signals their presence to the analyst. Of course, enactments themselves often go undetected by the analytic couple who experience the phenomenological *effect* of T(−H), which by its very definition creates confusion and difficulties in thinking in both members of the dyad.

For example, a patient operating under the sway of T(−H) may self-induce experiences of manic reparation in order to stop the bleeding-out of their representational capacity and the resulting inability to hold inner experience. Green describes this when writing about the dead mother complex, which involves these very same processes of negative hallucination of thinking. However, in the case of the dead mother, the object is not completely erased as it is "encapsulated". When contact with her is lost, a black hole is left behind by the de-cathexis, which, in the case of a dead mother, the depressed patient identifies with. As was discussed in Chapter 3, for Green, voids or black holes are created in the psyche in both the situations of the dead mother and T(−H). In the first case, black holes are created in place of a mother who is psychically dead to the subject, whose projected emotions are rendered lifeless by the encounter with the dead mother and reinternalized in this way;[2] In the second case, black holes are created in place of the elements of thinking that are subverted from within. One needs only to recall the scenes in the film *Eternal Sunshine of the Spotless Mind* where, as Joel's memories are being erased so he can stop thinking about Clementine, the visual imagery that corresponds to them begins to disappear. Instead of finding the relief he expects, he begins to feel panicked, as before the memories disappear, he experiences them once again and does not want to part with them. Under the direction of his image of Clementine, he projects the memories related to her into unrelated other memories, effectively creating bizarre objects while halting the process of de-cathexis. In other words, he protects his emotional attachment to her image by projecting it into other innocuous images. In the film, we see this when Joel takes Clem by the hand and leads her into his childhood memories where they can both hide. However, the neurosurgeon overseeing the whole process re-starts the erasure operation, and now begins to attack as many

DOI: 10.4324/9781003520740-5

of Joel's memories as he can, perhaps indicating that even when hidden in bizarre objects, the emotional registration of the memory of Clementine is still too painful without having to eliminate all of the images (thoughts) available in Joel's mind to construct her. Joel, a subject now caught in the grips of a radical de-cathexis, manically tries to fill in these newly created voids, by jumping from one childhood memory to another, as if attempting to restart the cathexis of his inner world. This is what Green (1986, 1999a) refers to as *passion*,[3] in patients often manifested in a frantic need to play, to imagine, or to think that is more compulsive than free. With this passion, the subject attempts to create "a piece of cognitive fabric which is destined to mask the hole left by the de-cathexis" (1986, p. 152). Paradoxically, this passion can often have the effect of keeping the object at a distance, and when the analyst is that object, he may countertransferentially experience being "hosed" by the patient's unrelenting or excessive verbiage or be overwhelmed by the patient's need for verbal or physical contact. At other moments he may feel intruded on by what he experiences as the patient's excessive playfulness or need to catch the analyst's eye. When enacted defensively, say the analyst asks an exploratory question rather than answering a patient's playful but unrelenting questioning in hopes of slowing her down, these countertransferential responses reproduce the same painful break of contact with the object that induces the creation of the black holes that then impel the patient into passionate reconstruction. Thus, the hyperbolic cycle detailed at the end of the last chapter is generated. When anxious Joel asks Dr. Mierzwiek if the memory erasing procedure carries any risk of brain damage, he is told, "well technically speaking, the operation *is* brain damage".

At a certain point in our work, Ms. S[4] began missing appointments with me deliberately. She also requested additional "emergency" sessions or re-scheduled set appointments. It did not take long to discover the meaning of this as it was perfectly conscious for Ms. S, who told me she wanted to know for herself whether or not the sessions meant anything to her. She planned them, and then missed or moved them purposely, in order to monitor herself afterwards to see if she felt anything in response. It was usually the case that she "felt nothing" apart from disorganization during the long hours on both sides of the session. Upon hearing this, I understood in a different light Ms. S's tendency, probably a compulsion, to pay me immediately after each session. Did she need to use a payment that included an email confirmation sent to both of us and funds moving from her account into mine to inscribe in her psyche the fact of having had a session that day, whether she attended or not? Was this a way of generating the sensation and capturing the experience of movement between something her and something me?

It is possible that when Ms. S created absences by missing appointments, experimenting with our session frequencies and re-scheduling sessions, she was attempting to generate a felt experience of absence with which to create a space for an idea of me/our session to form. In this sense, alpha-function was working in some rudimentary way and serving to bind negative with positive hallucinosis. It was as if she was trying to create in her mind the negative hallucination of the object, and in this way, a framework, a canvas, "a piece of cognitive fabric" onto which she might begin to hallucinate, imaginarize (Green, 1999b, p. 207) and know her thoughts. In her words, "I want to know if there is something I miss, then I will know if there is something there".

It is with some reservation that I will call this aforementioned scenario an enactment, but I will do so because despite the seemingly one-sided nature of the patient's behavior, in general the patient was responding to a chronic situation that had been enacted overtime between us where try as I did to be a container, I repeatedly functioned as a projective-identification denying object, or as Bion called it, and obstructive object (Bion, 1958, p. 136). As was described in Chapter 2, in my inability to dream Ms. S's communications to me, I responded from my position in PS (paranoid-schizoid) rather than D (depressive), and my interpretations, however symbolic they appeared to me at the time, functioned as defensive reprojections back into the patient of the emotional contents she was hoping I would be able to expand. In this way, on my side I enacted the role of her overly anxious parents and more fundamentally, the concretely anxious and obstructive internal object she had internalized through them. A chronic enactment had settled into a pattern of relating between us that cathected the hyperbolic loop of T(−H) until the enactment became acute, acted out on the patient's side through the canceled and re-scheduled sessions. Through the empty space created by the missing sessions, Ms. S attempted to recreate my presence, having been evacuated from her internal world for feeling intrusive and obstructive.

Transformations in negative hallucinosis and the enactment of pathological organizations

Mr. D

Mr. D insisted that I remove my mobile phone from my office in order to feel freer to speak with me candidly. He was certain that it had been bugged by members of "The Organization", who were trying to get to him through me. At night and during the day, most probably while he was in session with me, "they" ransacked his apartment. They inserted drives and empty folders into his laptops and followed him around upstairs when he moved through his apartment, or outside in a helicopter that was frequently flying over the city.

It was in the sixth month of a three times a week, face to face analysis when the phone situation seemed to come to a head. Previously, as with the case of his other persecutory hallucinoses, I attempted to explore the nature and details of his beliefs while being as careful as possible not to challenge them. As with other patients in acute paranoid states, I knew from experience that questioning the realness of these delusions when much of the personality was captured by them, including, as I detailed in Chapters 2 and 3, the objectalization function part and parcel of alpha-functioning, often led to my inclusion in the patient's delusion as a persecutor, or stimulated the patient to quit treatment altogether for want of someone who will hear them out without telling them they were crazy. So I always treaded carefully with Mr. D, noting to myself that when I did venture to question the veracity of his beliefs and offered alternative explanations, it tended to be in moments when I was feeling flooded by the content and the lack of emotional resonance between his words and my emotional experience. It was in those moments that I was the most anxious for his well-being. For months, I had been grappling with how to work with his psychosis, which did not seem to be diminishing in intensity despite the analytic work we did on the emotions that seemed to be fueling the heightened persecutory states. Mr. D struck me as a gentle man, who despite his soft-spokenness and friendly demeanor had an oafy appearance and way of carrying himself that I surmised, but that he did not suspect, could be intimidating to others who he noticed crossed the street when he walked by. Despite his once questioning me if I carried a concealed weapon or his off and on again nudging me to remove my mobile phone from my office, which I had repeatedly explained I needed nearby for both of our safety, I felt amazingly relaxed in his presence. I felt he was agreeable, enthusiastic about attending, and willing to speak openly even though he claimed he could not because of my phone. It took some time before I was able to put together my felt experience of relaxedness and self-confidence with his feeling that everyone around him was "false" and "inauthentic". What I grew to understand was that the patient was projecting into me a superior omnipotent object, while he himself was identified with the inferior persecuted subject. I think I took unconscious comfort in this projection and identified with it, as it kept me safe from the awareness of more dangerous feelings in the transference. But this understanding took many months to develop, and until then, both Mr. D and I were captured in what in retrospect I was able to think of as a transformation in both positive and negative hallucinosis. These (unconscious) phantasies of superiority and self-sufficiency form part of what Bion called "the rules" (1965, p. 254) of T(H), often manifest in a moralizing, pedagogical, and authoritarian attitude in the subject used to deny dependency on the object (Civitarese, 2015; Sandler, 2005, 2009). This phantasy was lived out unconsciously with the patient's projection and hallucination of me as superior to him (he often remarked on how much thinner I was to him, or how eloquent my words were in comparison to his, etc.) and my feeling fantastic, alert, and clear-headed most of the time.

At other moments, however, Mr. D, who was a member of a dark, underground esoteric music scene, spoke to me from up high about music in a way that felt pedagogical. He was also playful when he shared his ideas with me, and lively, and in many ways these discussions felt friendly and collaborative. But I also sensed that he looked down on me. He said he could surmise, by the looks of me, which bands I might listen to and instructed me on their inferior quality while being friendly about it. It was only one day when he spoke disparagingly about the Beatles that I felt something inside me give, and I began to question my upbeat analytic attitude and unusually playful demeanor with a man who was also suffering so much. Outside of our sessions, Mr. D's personal life was stalling, as he was unable to search for work on a computer he felt was constantly being tampered with and was trapped inside a tiny apartment for fear of being followed on the street.

My approach with Mr. D was as it is with any analytic patient in the sense of listening patiently, attentively, and empathically to whatever he brought to our sessions, hoping to stimulate and offer further thinking about the emotions that were consuming him and that often triggered his persecutory delusions. Things became more difficult countertransferentially when Mr. D entered sessions in an acute state of T(+H), at times handing me pieces of paper in which he scribbled frantic messages to me for fear of speaking out loud, or on the edge of explosion having spent a night besieged by the neighbors upstairs or the helicopters overhead. At these moments, bearing these emotions with him felt paralyzing and far from the fantastic and relaxed states I could otherwise feel in his presence. I became hyperattentive to his words and to the details of what he was describing, grasping at his logic and hoping to unlock him from the cage of totalitarian coherence by trying to speak to him rationally. When the sessions were not flooded with delusional material, however, I was able to recover my use of reverie and intuition and felt freer and more able to enlist his engagement in exploring his emotions. These moments eventually evolved into more clarity on both of our parts about what was happening in Mr. D's mind, though not without my eventually returning to the more alert and "fantastic" countertransference feelings described earlier. Over time I became better equipped to think of these feelings as signals. I am using the words "evolved" here deliberately because in line with Bion I consider these evolutions in O. That is, they are transformations from a state of total sensoriality, or total Reality, to T(+/−H), and back to O, or total sensorial Reality where depressive position understanding achieved through reverie and intuition is transformed, through the reemergence of anxiety, into an O yielding pleasure (or the fantastic feeling), at the expense of deeper understanding.

When immersed listening to Mr. D's T(+H), I often shifted from experiencing dry states of mind or blurriness, where I tried to make sense out of words that to my ear flowed meaninglessly one after the other, to visual states where images appeared in my mind that I brushed aside as merely amusing. I tended not to question these images at first, likely because they provided pleasure and helped me feel awake underneath the mass of disconnected content. I'd like to emphasize the involuntary nature of this countertransferential pushing away, or at least how unaware I was of its meaning, because I consider it symptomatic of a state of T(−H) where unconsciously deliberate attempts are made to denude experience of its meaning. I was concerned for Mr. D who in these moments could be visibly shaken, and I struggled to take in the bizarre content of his anxieties. Often, these were accompanied by physically defensive and embattled body posturing, which I barely noticed myself not reacting to. I also cared about Mr. D and liked being in his company, and I felt a certain amount of guilt for having difficulty staying connected to his stories when a link with anything that I could recognize as reality was missing. In between my stressful attentiveness and dry internal processing, I would see and ignore images, which later I could recognize from the films *Memento* and *Angel Heart*, both involving investigator protagonists who struggle against memory to unravel a crime that has been committed. In both cases, it is the protagonist himself, Leonard and Harry Angel/Johnny Favorite respectively, who have unknowingly committed the crimes they are now attempting to get to the bottom of. Of course, the prototype for these characters is the immortal Oedipus, who as both Freud and Bion described, and of whom I will write more in the next chapter, unknowingly commits the crime he later sets out to solve.

During a series of sessions following a midyear vacation where I needed to cancel a week of our appointments, Mr. D's fears about my cellphone reemerged, having gone underground for over a month. Mr. D became more adamant in his sessions against my having my phone inside the office, despite my having it far from view on my desk. His, until this moment, friendly advice that I get my phone checked out at the Apple store and obtain a certificate declaring it was clean from tracking devices, became less friendly and more insistent. During one of these moments, I felt extremely tired, having just felt fresh and awake only a few minutes earlier. It was at the beginning of the workday, and I had slept pretty well the night before. But quickly, I began to feel a heaviness weighing down my ability to think. I include these details because they were part of my self-observations at the time, and to me they are indicative of being induced into a state of $T(-H)$, where in my confusion, grasping at causes and effects that would shed light on my mental condition, I clung on to the facts of reality as pieces of evidence in solving the crime of who or what was drugging me. At some moment, listening to Mr. D go on about my phone, I became suddenly defensive and suggested that if he was so concerned about his and my devices, why did he not take his own laptop to get certified? Almost immediately I felt alarmed at having made such a hostile comment to Mr. D, but I was able to ascertain that I was feeling what Mawson (2019) termed "ontological anxiety", states of mind where the analyst is feeling captured by the patient's use of him in the transference.

Mawson's idea is important for understanding how the analyst must and can employ reverie in moments of such anxieties in order to move his reverie into a state of dreaming that can help formulate to himself and in turn, to the patient, containing words to give form and substance to the intensity of emotions experienced by both. For Mawson, an analyst experiences such ontological anxiety when he is feeling recruited into a role-relationship, where not only painful emotions are being evoked, but a disturbing calling into question is occurring, deep inside of himself, of who and what he is. In these moments, the analyst is unaware that he is having an experience where he is straining to take in the transference, and is usually feeling done-to, and with good cause, because what he fails to understand is that the patient is in the process of communicating something of the O of his experience. Put in field terms, the intersubjective field is undergoing a transformation in O, where the patient's beta-elements are being made to reside in the analyst, who resists this as if his sense of subjectivity depended on it. And in a sense, *it does*, since the analyst has to be receptive in these moments to allowing the patient's subjectivity, or the intersubjective analytic third of the field occupy his inner space without losing touch with himself. As such, countertransferential resistance portends a transformation in O that the analyst is well-advised to be receptive to. This resistance in the countertransference also relates to Wilson's (2020) description of countertransference as resistance *per excellence*, in that the analyst feels thwarted in his unconscious desire vis-à-vis the patient and resists being transformed into someone he does not wish the patient to see him as, or he himself does not wish to feel himself to be. So we might think of different levels to the analyst's resistance to being transformed by the patient's transference, passing through wishing to be seen differently than the patient sees him, and reaching into the analyst's state of *being* someone different than he knows himself to be in essence.

In this light, I became aware of unconsciously feeling hostile to Mr. D by experiencing my own countertransferential response to him. I came to sense that I was feeling unjustly accused of being a stooge of the Organization that had supposedly tapped my phone to get to him, and I felt that accusation on a concrete level. In my bones, so to speak, I felt that I was being experienced as dangerously hostile by Mr. D, as if I were an enemy, and I took a deep, at the time confusing to me, offense to this. I think even the word *offense* fails me here. It is the feeling of having one's basic sense of who one is erased, or in Green's term *effaced*, a word he uses when recalling the dead mother's impact on the child's psyche. My sense of subjectivity, from where the meanings of my words and demeanor originate, and are recognizable *to me as mine*, felt effaced. The things I said and the way I behaved, *for him*, operated as signs that pointed to something radically alien to how I felt myself to be. It was only when I heard and tasted the hostility in my suggestion to take his own device to the Apple store that I became aware of "murder" entering the analytic field in an important way. Likely it had been there all along, haunting the field between us like our own ghosts, underneath the disguise of my fantastic countertransference feelings and in the whispers he imagined at the other end of my phone line. I began to consider that our hostilities, mine and his, were related to a defensive imperative on both of our parts to hold on to our senses of who we were, now in direct danger of being killed off by the other.

This new awareness helped me see more clearly the chronic enactment that, in the form of a reaction formation, had been created between Mr. D and myself. Cassorla (2018), as I will explain further, refers to these types of chronic enactments as states of non-dreams-for-two, where patient and analyst are ensnared in an impasse without realizing it, characterized by reverie deprivation and acting out. With latent murderous hostility operating now as a selected fact, I could see what to the reader might have already been obvious—that Mr. D was terrified of me and thought that *I* would murder him. I became aware of the likelihood that the announcement of my vacation felt like a murderous attack on the tie that held us together, in the sense that Winnicott (1974) described in "Fear of breakdown". Like the infant in a state of absolute dependency, Mr. D was afraid that in the absence of the mother-infant bond that tied us together, he would fall prey to the agonies of contact with the object, and with that, reality. The sense that someone was constantly keeping tabs on him through my phone, I began to think, restored in his mind a feeling of being in constant contact with an object who was deeply interested in him and with whom he was forever linked (perhaps this contributes to the persecutory claustrophobic quality of these types of bonds). I also began to see how my upbeat mood, a reaction formation to my unconscious sense of hostility and fear, was fueling Mr. D's suspicion of me and making him more worried about who I was really working for, sensing abandonment in my inauthentic state. This inauthentic state of feeling fantastic and upbeat with Mr. D was the pleasurable discharge of a T(−H) where I was unable to represent to myself, under the weight of unconscious anxiety, what was actually occurring in the room or what Mr. D's now obvious communications to me were. Additionally, when I defensively called into question his delusional beliefs, I actually enacted the aggressor by attacking his subjectivity, his sense of who he was and what was happening to him, and realized the identity theft he feared he was the victim of through his electronic devices.

The other state of mind that was a factor of the T(−H) was the dry and empty non-receptive state, which usually lead to heightened anxiety in both of us. For me, being in this state of evacuating meaning until reaching a state of meaninglessness triggered, possibly as counterbalances, T(+H). These were in the form of images from films, images that I experienced as amusing and unrelated, that is, as bizarre objects. What I mean by this is that I would at times involuntarily withdraw into daydreaming perhaps as a means of obtaining some relief from the intense attention to his detailed persecutory narrations. I simultaneously felt a resistance to taking the images of my daydreaming seriously enough to relinquish the pleasure they yielded and to put them to work, so to speak. Now, more aware of the emotions in the room with Mr. D, I was able to get a clearer picture of his inner world and connect them to these T(+H) from *Memento* and *Angel Heart* that from this new vertex transformed into reveries that could now be put to use (transformed) as a dream.

As he labored to tell me how, once again, as he was sitting down in front of his MacBook to compose a cover letter for a job application, he got distracted into hunting down, reprograming, and erasing suspicious files in his hard drive in search of the origins of something unusual on his screen, I began to imagine (dream) Mr. D as Leonard or Harry Angel, who unknowingly causes the crime he then tries to solve. I saw him in my mind in a confused and terrified state, playing coding whack-a-mole with ghosts he sensed in bits and images on his screen, deleting files and causing damage he later did not remember or understand he had caused but was bent on getting to the bottom of. Mr. D, during the course of these first six months, went through half a dozen new laptops, all thrown away when they became unserviceable. At the same time, and in the same light, I began to take notice of how my interpretations to him—which I had failed to see where not correctly formulated and used as a way of diminishing my own anxiety—were contributing to the crime of mind theft I was trying to help him solve. Mr. D complained vociferously that "they" were not allowing him to organize his thinking and sabotaging his own ability to know what was real. My interpretations, enacted defensively and in that way, poorly timed, robbed him of his own tenuous self-understanding, without offering him a more convincing understanding of what was happening in his mind (his computer, his apartment).

With these understandings more consciously available to me, I was able to wait more patiently for a moment when he appeared to be open to understanding in the service of diminishing his pain. As noted earlier, because my state—and I would add the state of the analytic field between us—was submerged in T(−H), it took some time for me to realize that I was interpreting in moments when Mr. D was in evacuative/projective mode. More attentive now to his receptive mode of psychic functioning I found an opening to say that I wondered if it made sense to think that he had to believe all of these terrible things were happening to him because that helped him organize to himself what he was feeling, which protected him from a deeper fear of becoming disorganized and ill again when he was overcome by emotions. I was surprised that Mr. D did not resist this understanding, and I was able to add that the "Organization" he was telling me about sounded a lot like the neighborhood bullies that tormented him in childhood, as well as the high school teachers and the guidance counselor (later, me) who undermined his belief in himself. The comparison felt as clear as day when neither of us was afraid of the other and open to mutual influence. At the very end of the hour, Mr. D returned to his persecutory anxiety, but when these reappeared as the weeks and months went on, they were intermingled with increasing moments of clarity and his own qualification of them as "paranoid". He also began feeling less depressed, likely due to feeling more supported by the shift in my analytic attitude, despite frequent relapses into his paranoid beliefs. For my part, maintaining that attitude became more sustainable as I experienced more faith (F) in the organizing capacity of the better-timed interpretations of his paranoia. This faith felt most important given the intensity of the material and my fear that Mr. D could regress rapidly and seemingly unpredictably.

T(−H) and psychosis

This understanding of the function of the paranoid delusion is in line with established literature on the subject. I have in mind here De Masi's (2006) understanding of paranoia as a process of withdrawal from painful psychic reality of the loss of the object (the parents) into a fantasy that distances the subject from the abandonment and replaces it with, if not pleasure, then omnipotent excitement with overtones of masochism and persecution. Steiner's pathological organizations as psychic retreats also comes to mind. Both follow the logic of Freud's and Bion's reconstruction in omnipotent fantasy of the fractured relationship between the ego and the sense of reality. For Steiner, as well as for Bion, the subject attacks his ability to perceive reality, or in the terms of my proposal in this book, he transforms outer and inner reality through negative hallucinosis into meaningless, contentless matter, breaking it up into fragments and allowing him to "turn a blind eye" (Steiner, 2018) to the emotional pain of absolute dependency on a reality essentialized as loss (the lost object, unsymbolized, is experienced as total Reality). This psychic retreat helps the subject avoid contact then with real people in real life situations that would bring up this real and internal pain. But this destruction of the means of contact with reality, i.e., perception, produces the experience of mental fragmentation and an incoherent experience of the world, creating unbearable confusion and anguish, and furthering the need to create a stronger pathological organization (the delusion) into which retreat. The delusion is then the medication against the pain it contributes to creating (De Masi, 2006). The incoherent experience of the world, of course, is paradoxical given that the paranoid beliefs are meant to create a coherence where otherwise unbound, unmentalized stimuli reign free in the subject's mind. Returning to Bion, a delusion is in fact a "beta-screen" (Bion, 1962b, p. 290). According to him,

> (T)hat is to say that if the personality lacks the apparatus that would enable it to "think" thoughts but is capable of attempting to rid the psyche of thoughts in much the same way as it rids itself of accretions of stimuli, then reversal of alpha-function may be the method employed. Instead of sense impressions being changed into alpha-elements for use in dream thoughts and unconscious waking thinking, the development of the contact-barrier is replaced by its destruction. This is effected by the reversal of alpha-function so that the contact-barrier and the dream thoughts and unconscious waking thinking, which are the texture of the contact-barrier are turned into alpha-elements, divested of all characteristics that separate them from beta-elements and are then projected thus forming the beta-screen.
>
> (idem, p. 293)

That is to say, the contact-barrier that would form that double-limit between unconscious and preconscious, separating out beta-elements from alpha-elements and transforming the sensorial experience into the symbolic, dream narrative that undergirds thinking, is destroyed as part of the mental apparatus' attack on perception. This is meant to impede not as much the ability to think unbearable but formulated thoughts, as in repression, but to block the registering of perceptions in any structure conducive to pictogrammic, and later ideogrammic form leading to thinking in the first place.[5] In the process, a situation of symbolic equation (Segal, 1957) ensues where the (rudimentary) symbol (any abstraction away from the thing) is equated with the thing symbolized. In the case of Ms. S discussed earlier and in Chapters 2 and 3, the words I said were experienced, eventually by the both of us, as exactly the same words she said, with no referent to other meanings, understandings, ambiguities that had been present in my mind when I formulated them to her. With Mr. D, the meaning of his persecutory beliefs told a story that was flatly true in his mind, with no referent to any inner self-accusatory thoughts or feelings. The T(−H) is effectuated by stripping away from the alpha-elements anything that would distinguish them from beta-elements, which is Bion's way of saying that any images that might be formed as a way of containing and elaborating the frustration felt by the impact of the emotion (the sensation) is aborted or destroyed, so that meaning is either foreclosed or strangled at birth. But the remaining beta-elements that have been evacuated in the process cohere in the form of a screen, a delusion, not in an attempt to give meaning—this process was sabotaged—but to keep the mind together by arranging the beta-elements in a form that has some sort of coherence, even if mystifying. It is this, then, that the subject tries to make sense of, which it has no way of doing without inferring nefarious motivations in line with the "Lego blocks" that even now, realigned in different configurations, contain the contours and shading of the terrifying impulses they were meant to transport on their way out. Bergstein gives us a compelling description of this. When writing about T(H), he states

> The patient's transformation of the emotional experience is now so mutilated that if there ever was an unconscious phantasy, it is now unknowable. It is utterly dispersed in space, chaotic in a way that cannot be grasped in terms of time and space. Its original shape is almost completely lost.
>
> (Bergstein, 2019, p. 9)

The paranoid belief, then, is an attempt to gather these mutilated parts into some stabilizing form, the beta-screen, that would make sense to the subject, which is not to say that it has Meaning. In fact, this is what torments the subject the most—the meaninglessness of it all. Why is he, such a good and honest person, someone who has done nothing wrong, of all people, being tormented in this way? And how could so many people know about him and be so involved in his destruction? These are questions the paranoid subject asks, but not without concluding the obvious, which, to repeat, does not amount to Meaning. Meaning, of course, must be shared, is not idiosyncratic, but belongs to the realm of what Bion refers to as "common-sense". Bion is clearest on this subject in *Attention and Interpretation* (1970), when writing about the mystic and the group:

> For example, the psychotic patient does not always behave as if he is incapable of symbol formation. Indeed, he often talks or behaves as if he is convinced that certain actions, which to me are innocent of any symbolic significance, are obviously symbolic. They mean, apparently obviously, some message which is of personal and particular concern to him. This "meaning" is quite different from the meaning one assumes to lie behind a constant conjunction that is public and not private to one individual. The former is, and appears to belong to, a private communication made by God (or Devil or Fate); when the psychotic symbol is met with in practice its significance seems to be less that it symbolizes something, more that it indicates that the patient is in private rapport with a deity or demon. The symbol, as it is usually understood, represents a conjunction which is recognized by a group to be constant; as encountered in psychosis it represents a conjunction between a patient and his deity which the patient feels to be constant.
>
> (idem, pp. 275–276)

The beta-screen/paranoid belief is an attempt to organize experience, to bind the unbound and frenzied energies that are released in T(−H)'s attempts at unburdening the mind from the elements that would construct thinking and produce further frustration. I mentioned earlier Winnicott's (1974) insights, outlined in his paper, "Fear of Breakdown", that the illness itself is a defense against the fear of experiencing the breakdown of the mother-infant bond supposed to have occurred already when the subject was in a state of absolute dependence but did not have the capacity to represent it to himself. Even when the beta-screen or pathological organization is felt to be painful and persecutory in itself, as with Mr. D, it is preferable to the anguish that is feared if reality is faced on its own terms since this threatens to trigger an internal, unbearable emotional reality that the subject has to endure alone. For Winnicott, as Ogden (2014) explains in his illuminating reading of this paper, the primitive agonies that become unbearable—in Mr. D's case these are the agonies of the loss of a sense of what is real and a loss of the capacity to relate to objects (idem, p. 53), triggered by my announcing my vacation dates—are only so because the tie with the mother is not there to hold the infant through these agonies. The subject, now alone in facing them, *creates* the experience of loss of reality in order to self-hold and not be swept away passively by this loss of reality and object-closeness contingent on this early bond. He takes matters into his own hands, so to speak, bringing the painful loss into his sphere of omnipotence and control. Mr. D, now in his mid-40s, had had a life replete with starts and stalls due to the tenacities of his will, intelligence, and T(H) and was still to grieve his wife's abandonment and the death of a mother who, despite her schizophrenia, was a beloved caretaker to whom he was devoted and on whom, I suspected, he felt emotionally dependent. For Mr. D, there was a lot at stake in writing a cover letter and stepping out into the world alone.

Now, while this was the way his painful delusion functioned to protect him from further pain, it is intriguing how the contours of the pathological beliefs trace the psychodynamics and the metapsychology involved. First, that it is "the Organization" that he identifies as a front for what in reality is an unconscious defensive "pathological organization". The unnerving sense that something is being organized around him replaces the uncanny knowledge that something is being reorganized within him. Secondly, the belief that files are being erased from his hard drive, leaving him in a state of confusion (not knowing or understanding) and with an inability to organize his thinking and to write a cover letter (to think), while he himself is the one erasing these crucial files and damaging his "hard drive" through attacks on linking. Gradually it seemed clearer that what he was narrating to me unbeknownst to himself was the ejection of the Lego pieces (Meltzer & Scolmati, 2009) of his thoughts (his files being erased) forming bizarre objects (his tampered computer, the neighbors upstairs, the helicopters, and my cell phone) carrying, in inverted and loosely related form, fragments of the whole of an internal process of T(−H) where the files/ideas/internal images of his experience—that is, thinking about his internal and external predicament—are corrupted and erased through the destruction of his own ability to think through his emotions. What remains in the aftermath is nothingness, confusion, enigma. In unconsciously creating the situation that then begged the explanation, Mr. D was controlling the implosion of the loss of his capacity to think (to know what is real, to relate to objects) by actualizing a fantasy that his thinking was being attacked by others, others who stalked him like a ghost and would not abandon him as I did on the weekends and on vacations.

Transformations in negative hallucinosis and non-dreams-for-two

The shift in my interpretative attitude, facilitated by my regaining the ability to dream the session, helped me step out of an enactment co-sustained with Mr. D where, with my cell phone as my avatar I was endangering his ability to think his own thoughts, which he could not speak without danger that I would turn them against him to rob him of whatever self-representation his understandings provided. The connection between T(H) and enactment has been made by Roosevelt Cassorla (2018), in his study of chronic and acute enactments in relation to dreaming and non-dreaming. Dreaming the emotional stream of the session usually reflects the ability to effect transformations in O and K, the totality of sensorial experiences and the ability to process them through rudimentary imagery qua alpha-functioning. T(−H), however, specifically involve a reversal of the dreaming activity that comprises thinking as described earlier. They can be thought of as states of non-dreaming and are fertile ground for the development of chronic and acute enactments (Cassorla, 2018). When mired in negative hallucinosis, enactment can take an insidious form, chronic though undetected until a disruption, perhaps in the form of an acute enactment or a hallucination, takes place. T(−H), whether or not they are accompanied by T(+H), can induce states of non-dreaming that serve as a source for the actualization of traumatic emotions and negative (absent) objects in the transference and in the analytic field, perpetuating an enactment (Barahona, 2020). Cassorla describes *enactment* as something that

> occurs unconsciously, and involves both analyst and patient, who perform current situations or archaic fantasies, reflections of transferential or countertransferential fears and hopes, sometimes enacting real or fantasized traumatic situations from the past. The enactment is the consequence of the impossibility of externalizing these situations, or unconscious fantasies linked to them, through verbal symbolization. They are often thus regressive interactions, and one of their characteristics is that they involve both the analysand and the analyst.
>
> (2001, p. 1156)

We see in this definition that the process involves a failure or obstruction of the capacity to receive and interpret emotions symbolically and that it usually involves both members of the dyad without the source of the obstruction needing to be specified. Clinically, it is of course the analyst who, as "guardian of the frame" (Bleger, 1967), is tasked with the role of helping the analytic duo reflect on and process the emotions that are being avoided or enacted within and between them. Even though responsibility lies with the analyst, how the remediation process is initiated is less clear, though it usually begins with the analyst working through moments of enactment by recovering the capacity to dream what has not been dreamt, and by finding images and words to serve as containing metaphors. This is made possible through the analyst's use of himself as a container conducive to reverie where these images, and then thoughts that will prove necessary for the working through process, are allowed to materialize in the analyst's mind in a form suitable for meaningful communication to the patient (Barahona, 2020).

When these moments of enactment occur, they may be used by the analyst as signals that enable him to retroactively detect situations, often long-stretches of time, where T($-$H) have been deadening emotions in states of otherwise high stimulation between himself and the patient and impeding his ability to find them in reverie. I am deliberately using the words "find them in reverie" because I do not think it is possible for the analyst *not* to have reverie, and that states otherwise described as reverie deprivation or -R (Civitarese & Ferro, 2022)[6] might be better thought of as moments of -F (faith) where, giving into despair, the analyst has lost his faith in the analytic relevance of his total experience, in this case the total experience of being psychically dry. I am reminded here of Bion's account (related in Chapter 1) of standing in front of the dry river channel of the Luce on the eve of battle without intuiting the imminence of the fog that would obscure the path forward for his tanks. The obscuring fog was a transformation of the same invariants that had previously composed a full river, but Bion, in a state of anguish before battle, could only experience the dryness and not intuit this connection to reestablish causality in his mind and get a sense of the larger picture.

In moments like these, the analyst's ability for bi-ocularity (De Masi, 2015), where one "eye" remains focused on understanding and interpretation while the other "eye", unfocused preserves a space "for something else" (Birksted-Breen, 2016, p. 26), has been impaired. When not impaired, this space may be inhabited by reverie. Otherwise, on one level, patient and analyst are working in a way that passes for productive; on another level the work may be saturated with gnawing but ignorable feelings of staleness, lack of progress, fear, anxiety, dread, irritation, or indifference. The eye that would remain unfocused and in that way open to the emotional and visual impressions that constitute dreaming the session (Bion, 1958–1979, p. 118) remains overly-focused and closed (Barahona, 2022). In this way, instead of a dream being dreamt by the analyst of the patient's unconscious experience communicated intersubjectively, a *non-dream-for two* is created, essentially, a nightmare from which the possibility of acting out may offer if only a superficial and illusory respite.

T(–H) and dreaming

In describing non-dreams-for-two, Cassorla (2018) explains that he has in mind a potential dream that has not yet taken place but that could take place—that is, could be dreamed—if it were to find another dreaming mind that could function as a container. Part of the problem occurs when the emotional intensity of the session is such that neither mind is able to adequately think and process the emotions communicated via words and behavior as symbols, that is, representations of sensorial experience in the field between the patient and analyst and within each one of them. It is of course the analyst's responsibility to be the symbolizer-in-chief, so to speak, and work toward containment of the emotions so that they can be translated into verbal form and communicated back to the patient who understands them as parts of himself not to be terrified of as if they were ghosts, which of course they are. The idea here is to help the patient (and analyst) repatriate the ghost. The patient, explains Cassorla, in unconscious phantasy, through the subtleties of their interactions with the analyst, places parts of himself, his objects, and his inner relations, within the analyst who is then seen in a distorted manner and is reacted to as such (2018, p. 3). We would add here that in enactment, the analyst also *reacts* as such. But the analyst's enacted identification aside, this process describes the back and forth of projective identification as communication (see Bion, 1958), one of Bion's extensions of Melanie Klein's theory, without which the analyst would have meager information about the patient's inner world to be able to communicate back something of value that the patient could accept.

When projective identifications are massive, however, exceeding their ability to communicate (or the analyst's capacity to transform them into communications through his alpha-function), they are experienced mostly in their sensorial form, denuded of discernible meaning and mostly as "undigested facts" (Bion, 1958–1979, p. 90), causing pain or even pleasure in the analyst but eluding his understanding. In these moments we would say that the container has broken or ceased to function and is now prone to acting in reverse, transforming itself into the contained (the projected elements experienced as facts) seeking a container in the patient, who duly resists and projects back or becomes more confused and unintegrated. In essence, series of these evacuations, projections, and introjections are what comprise the microprocesses within T(−H). When the container-contained configuration is functioning adequately, as I will describe later, the analyst is able to think through the emotions and access his imagination, intuition, and creativity and dream a dream, the latter composing a narrative that can function as an effective "cover letter" for the patient's inner experience. But, Cassorla writes,

> if the alpha-function is damaged and the container is unable to transform external and internal perceptions into something that passes for thought, we find ourselves with dysfunctional configurations where the analytic dyad cannot dream adequately . . . (resulting) in sterility or rigidity of thought that can be referred to as "non-dreams", the raw material for what will be described later on as "enactment".
>
> (2018, p. 3)

When an acute enactment occurs, the analyst has an opportunity, if he is able to recover his symbolic dreaming capacity, to discern whether or not it is the end result of a silent, ongoing, and therefore chronic enactment. If so, this enactment has likely been silent as a result of T(−H), where gradually the dynamic between external reality and psychic reality has ceased to function, leading to a symbolic equation of psychic realities into one complete O, which is experienced but cannot be reflected on or thought about to be detected. T(−H) is the diametrical opposite of dreaming, in as far as it is opposed to the use of symbols and works actively to dismantle them, whereas dreaming is symbolization par excellence. In this vein, Civitarese (2014) suggests we think of symbolism "as a gradient that goes from the symbolic equation to the symbol . . . from the proto-symbol of projective identification with the object to the concept" (p. 78). The brutal road from O to thinking then is paved with stones of denser to more abstract consistency, comprised of an admixture of beta and alpha-elements, every step of the way distancing the subject from immediate sensorial reality. It is dreaming that facilitates the paving of this road to thinking. We might say, then, that at the heart of the difference between Freud's and Bion's theories of dreaming lies the fact that for the former, the dream is the royal road to the unconscious; that is, for Freud, dreams are formed out of symbolic representations of childhood wishes that are disguised and hidden from the ego to protect sleep. For Bion, the emphasis is on the symbolizing process, and therefore, the dream is the royal road to *reality* (Sandler, 2005), "the way the mind thinks the real, 'O'" (Civitarese, 2014).

Thus far in this chapter and in the previous ones, I have been using the verb "dreaming" as synonymous with the waking processing of the psychic reality of the analytic pair in imagistic form. This requires the analyst's faith (F) in the use of his reverie as a vehicle for intuition and the recasting of the passive reverie images and sensations into the form of a dream narrative. As I mentioned before, Bion's theory of dreaming departed from Freud's, although I think the extent to which it did is debatable. There is a way in which one can read Bion's later insights in Freud. Freud's dream theory is illuminated in a different way when Bion's ideas act as selected facts to reorganize the emphases, or as vertices from which to shine a darker light on an unappreciated angle. So while Freud saw dreams as the protector of sleep, both disguising and fulfilling unconscious wishes, Bion (1958–1979) came to see dream-work as performing a digestive function that allowed the individual to suffer emotional experience, while at the same time, enriching his unconscious in a way that allowed him to imbue life with meaning. Freud's dream-work became Bion's dream-work-α, emphasizing the metabolizing and aesthetic functions contained within the distortion and censorship. From this vertex, displacement and condensation could be noted for their role in creating symbols and representation. Ultimately, Bion began using dreaming and alpha-function interchangeably (Abel-Hirsch, 2019). In this way, dreaming becomes linked to the selection, storing, and transformation of conscious and unconscious emotional material while the individual is both awake and asleep. Dreaming operates around the clock in the same manner as breathing and digestion (Cassorla, 2018). Thus, we can speak of the awake interaction between patient and analyst as dreaming or non-dreaming, depending on the symbolic capacity of the field formed by the two.

T(−H), enactment, and the container-contained relation

An acute enactment, as when I suggested to Mr. D that he take his own computer to the Apple store, signals the presence of an ongoing, undetected chronic enactment, which in turn is a sign to the analyst that he has not been functioning as a proper container for the patient's unmetabolized psychic experiences. Dreaming can only happen in a container—in fact, it may be argued that dreaming is what creates the container—and when non-dreaming replaces dreaming, instead of a container there is a void. The manifest content is concrete, yielding few if any associations, revealing itself to be a hallucination impersonating a dream (Bergstein, 2019). When in the analytic process, the analyst's dreaming repeatedly fails, and he is unable to dream the patient's unconscious communication, contact with the patient's projected internal object may pre-figure a behavioral enactment that discharges or evacuates the uncontained emotional experience (Brown, 2018), so that the relation with the negative object (the void) is actualized in the experience of the negative container.

Bion's theory of container-contained was first mentioned in "The Development of Schizophrenic Thought" written in 1956, and then developed more fully as a concept in *Learning from Experience* written in 1962. Here, he pulls into the bi-personal field what for Melanie Klein had already been a function of projective identification, namely, the modification of the infant's emotions through their sojourn in the mother's psyche. Bion saw this situation as being *commensal*, that is, when the container-contained relationship is working smoothly, evolution and psychic growth occurs in both minds, as can be seen by the dyad's growing ability to tolerate doubt and learn from experience. For the analyst as a container, this means his growing ability to "remain integrated, yet lose rigidity" (1962b, p. 359) in a way that frees memory and desire in the service of reverie, allowing a re-construal of past experiences into new ideas. This leads to growth in the ability to represent new emotional realities, a stronger capacity to repress represented emotions, and with these the expansion of the conscious and unconscious areas of experience (Barahona, 2020).

"When disjoined or denuded of emotion" says Bion of the conjoinment between container-contained, "they diminish in vitality, that is, approximate to inanimate objects" (1962b, p. 356). Here we have the inanimate pseudo-emotional state of hallucinosis, for example, one of T(+H) leading to T(−H) and -K. In the *Memento* and *Angel Heart* reverie examples in the case of Mr. D, I had become accustomed to pushing away the *wild thoughts* (Bion, 1977a, p. 175) that constituted my memories from those films as amusing but irrelevant, foreclosing their entry into a container where they would have developed emotionally and informed my experience of Mr. D, which included my role in an enactment as the investigator who, through my unnoticed mistimed and defensive interpretations, was causing the crime I was trying to investigate. Rather than increased understanding and relief, there was a palpable feeling of incremental dread, which as Bion writes, is terrifying because the failure of dream-work renders it nameless (Bion, 1958–1979, p. 49).

Concluding thoughts: on finding one's ghost

In the aforementioned descriptions of how an acute enactment can signal the undetected presence of a larger, chronic enactment and how this in turn often results from continuous processes of T(−H), a pattern emerges where it becomes clear that it takes two for a T(−H) to have a clinical effect. While, as in any hallucinatory state, it begins in the mind of one person and can be contained within it, clinically T(−H) form in a dialectic of thinking and non-thinking between the two members of the dyad where the flow of alpha-functioning is reversed under the pressure of unrepresented emotional experience by the mind that is experiencing the most anxiety in the room at the moment. This is the mind that is most engaged in expelling beta-elements and in recruiting the other in the process. Just as the container-contained dialectic is what leads to thinking through experience, and learning from it as a result, T(−H) dissolves the container-contained dialectic and creates a merger of the (un)contained, a dual O, but an O that the pair is *affected by* rather than shares. Merger is *not* the same as unison, the latter being closer to at-one-ment, to use Bion's term for that which occurs when the analytic couple is able to dream within a productive container-contained dialectic. Therefore, a healthy container-contained dialectic leads to a dialectic of sameness and difference, true atonement (see Civitarese, 2019 on this). T(−H) on the other hand, leads to *un*learning from experience, rather than learning. This model of learning or unlearning from the successful or unsuccessful experiences of projective identification reminds me of Pichon-Rivière's (1956–1957) ideas on the link and what he calls spiral process learning.[7] For Pichon-Rivière, the *link* is a complex structure that includes subject, object, and the relationship between them, internal and external. *Vínculo*, or link, then refers contemporaneously to interpersonal as well as internal object relations (Neri, 2009, p. 50). In terms of two subjects linked together, each one unconsciously assigns a role to the other and exerts pressure on him to identify with that role. Once unconsciously identified in his role, the other continuously incorporates it in his response, and so on, externalizing that internal object relation. We see what happens then when the function of the link is to negativize inner experience. What had been an internal reality, with potential for being thought about (because being internal, the subject can appreciate it at a distance through inwardly directed attention) becomes an external reality that cannot be thought about, only experienced (has become a bizarre object). In effect, what was unconscious to both members now becomes indistinguishable from external reality. In ordinary cases, this formulation approximates what Ogden (2004) calls the analytic third and is what in Bionian terms we would call a share*able* O, which in Bion's clinical recommendations the analyst strives to inhabit. Ideally, the analyst makes contact with this unconscious reality of the field when he is able to intuit the ineffable elements through immersion in the raw experience of this third and from the vertex of the waking dream function of his reverie. Paradoxically, this would be the area of experience where each subject is most alive to themselves, yet, unrepresented remains a place haunted by the ghosts of their unlived lives (Ogden, 2014, 2022), a transformation in negative hallucinosis of the self. In the consulting room, each subject, not quite truly a subject until these realizations can be borne out, lives a life they do not often realize is marked by the ghost of the other on to whom they have likewise projected their own.

This is more so the case when the container is strained, and the bulk of what is transferred in the interchange is no longer in the main alpha-elements and the alpha-function but the opposite, beta-elements and the reversal of alpha-functioning, as an anxiety relieving function of the mind(s) in the field. The link, and the field itself becomes negatively hallucinated (see Barahona, 2022). In this way the field becomes composed of two people doing to each other rather than fostering the psychoanalytic experience of mutual awareness of the other.

As I have tried to show in the case of Mr. D in this chapter and Ms. S in Chapters 2 and 3, it is incumbent upon the analyst to allow himself, in the process of analyzing his patient, the eventuality, if he can face it, of running into his own ghost when searching for the perpetuator of the crimes he suspects the patient is committing alone. Bion himself feared running into his own ghost if he returned to the Amiens-Roye Road, yet return he did, 40 years later, on a train with Francesca. He returned again and again, in *The War Diaries*, *Amiens*, *The Long Weekend*, and his later papers, including importantly, *On Arrogance*. In this paper, returning to the scene of the crime is part of the analyst's journey to the patient's and his own lived experience. I write about the importance of *On Arrogance* in the next chapter where I continue to make the point that recognition of T(−H) and their ubiquitous presence in enactments is paramount to taking the first strivings in the direction of bringing the ghost back home and restoring the psychoanalytic functioning of both minds at play. Only then can we accomplish what for Bion was the goal of psychoanalysis, that is, to introduce the patient, but here we must also add the analyst, to the most important people they are ever likely to have dealings with, namely, themselves (Bion, 1976, p. 63).

Notes

1 Parts of this chapter were adapted from Barahona, R. (2020) Living the Non-Dream: An Examination of the Links Between Dreaming, Enactment, and Transformations in Hallucinosis. *Psychoanalytic Quarterly* 89:689–714.
2 Jed Sekoff offers an interesting take on this concept of Green's, noting that "dead mother" is a misnomer, and suggests we think of her as more a "zombie" mother, more "undead" than "dead". As dead, she could be mourned, but as undead, we have the lifeless state in both the internal object and the subject's emotions in relation to her. In this case, we would not have a black hole in place of the live mother representation, but rather an extremely dense "point", a "centrifuge object", much like the hyperdense core of a star before it implodes into a black hole. It is less a "dead object" and more an object that is deadening. See Sekoff, 1999, p. 121. In Kohon, 1999.
3 See also Reed & Baudry, 2005.

4 This is the patient I began describing in Chapter 2.
5 This was also discussed in the previous chapter with reference to Meltzer's term dismantling.
6 Interestingly, Civitarese and Ferro relate -R to the dead mother, which they refer to as "a mother without reverie" (2022, p. 68).
7 It is interesting that both Bion and Pichon-Rivière, who presumably never heard of each other, both referred to these linking processes as experiences of "learning".

Chapter 5

The arrogance of transformations in negative hallucinosis. More clinical implications

Transformations in negative hallucinations, as we have seen in the previous chapters, involve the capture of the patient's and the analyst's thinking processes, which in Bionian terms refer to the interplay between sensoriality, affect, imagination, and language in the creation of representations. These processes are subjugated to the contrary functions of discharge of psychical tension through excessive evacuation leading up to the inability to represent experiences. In the consulting room, this includes the experiences generated in the here and now within the dyad. Naturally, these moments in an individual's or the analytic couple's psychic life are both contextual and circumscribed. While T(−H) can be said to be ubiquitous at least in the sense of providing the "negative" (in Green's meaning of *the negative*, explained in Chapters 2 and 3) to normal "positive" representational life and in the pathological functioning of otherwise well-functioning people, the term is not meant to describe the broad functioning of individuals who employ T(−H), unless we are speaking of people in whom the psychotic parts of their personalities hold sway over the non-psychotic parts. In other words, in most cases T(−H) is employed in specific moments where the emotional experience undergirding unconscious phantasy cannot be contained by the binding interplay of primary and secondary processes that comprise alpha-functioning (see Grotstein, 2007). As a result, the primitive defensive maneuvers of radical de-cathexis and disobjectalization are activated to negatively hallucinate a solution, a solution that devolves into a greater problem. When de-cathexis of the painful representation (of the experience with the object) for the purpose of neutralizing the affect[1] proves not enough, the functions of cathexis and objectalization themselves are next to go, foreclosing the eventuality of reencountering the intolerable object. When this occurs, the patient's ability to understand and hold emotional reality in the face of frustration becomes handicapped, and the anguish that is left unrepresented in its wake is dealt with by continued attempts at dismantling the thinking that links the ego to intolerable reality. As I will explain next, this is often accompanied by what André Green has called *passion* (Green, 1999a, 2005). Both the dismantling of thinking as well as passion play into what Bion (1958) described as *arrogance*, a state where the analyst and patient, singularly or together, can be said to be living in the non-dream state of T(−H).

DOI: 10.4324/9781003520740-6

The conversation

Ms. C is a woman who has spent her entire adult life feeling "dead" inside, like a "ghost", begrudgingly and resentfully carrying on with work and relationships with a sense that the excitement and desire she felt nascent in her teen years had been squashed out of existence by her tyrannical father. She was acutely concerned that the feeling of being alive would continue to elude her for the remainder of her life. As such, she was deeply depressed and tended to act out, at times violently, toward those close to her.

Ms. C began her session worried, describing an interaction she had had the previous day with one of her managers at work that was still agitating her, threatening to push her to the brink of despair. At the end of a meeting, the manager hurried Ms. C to the door, instantly making her feel anxious that she had somehow done something to make her manager, who she cared for deeply, upset with her. Despite the manager's explanation that she hurried her because she knew my patient needed to be at another meeting, Ms. C was left unsettled. Having just returned from vacation, she speculated that her manager's actions had to do with feelings she must have had about Ms. C's being away from her job. The morning of the session I'm about to relate, she had met with her manager again to ask if she was disappointed in her. Taken aback, the manager responded that she wasn't, but when pressed by my patient on her feelings about being away from her job, the manager did admit to some disappointment *about that*, but said she generally felt okay about it. Her manager went on to explain that there was no connection between those feelings and her reasons for rushing the patient out of their meeting. Nevertheless, Ms. C made it a point to let her manager know how much she valued their relationship and how conscientious she was about the impact of the time she had been away on vacation. She told me she was concerned about fraying this very valuable relationship and wanted to make sure she fixed anything about it that might have been damaged.

In session, Ms. C told me she was certain her manager had repressed the connection between her disappointment and the act of rushing her out of the room, but that the connection was there. This kind of certainty appeared elsewhere in Ms. C's interpretation of other people's malevolence toward her and is a hallmark of T(H). My sense was that what was transpiring in Ms. C's experience with this manager was an example of positive hallucinosis, where Ms. C needed the manager's anger to be a reality in order to contain something of her own unrecognized emotions. In this way she could effectuate a manic reparation to magically restore a love object she felt in danger of losing because of a phantasized attack.

It was not lost on me that I too had been away on vacation for two weeks, returning only the week prior, and that leading up to my vacation Ms. C had suddenly and abruptly canceled two weeks of her analysis to go on holiday, having been confused about the days that I would be away. Even though we had planned on stopping mid-August on a specific date as usual, at the beginning of that month Ms. C thought I was leaving straight away and that we had no more planned sessions. All of this was realized in the final moments of what turned out to be the last session before the break, an emotionally fraught, and not adequately processed final minutes, where my "see you next Monday" turned into "See you in one month . . .?" I felt a sudden, unexpected loss. Part of the reason for this had to do with my having made sure we had discussed our dates thoroughly, sensing her tentativeness about confirming them, a tentativeness I now regretted not having explored more fully. In any case, a reality had been established leading up to the start of the month, presumably for both of us but definitively for me, a reality that was suddenly made unreal and disorienting. When we resumed our sessions in the fall, she remembered none of these discussions.

I recognized the transference implications, then, in my patient's anxiety about having disappointed her manager, but keeping in mind Ms. C's penchant for intellectualization and the difficulty she often had with abstracting one situation into another, I decided to focus only on the concrete scene of her interaction with her manager. This was where the surface level of her anxiety was concentrated. I said to Ms. C,

> You were anxious that you might have disappointed, and in that way hurt your manager, with whom your relationship matters so much. I think you might have wanted some reassurance that she felt that you were a good, conscientious person who took her into consideration, and not a "bad" person, who "left people hanging".

I was using the language of sessions earlier in the week, where the feeling of "leaving people hanging" had come up not only in relation to how she canceled two weeks of sessions with me, but to a friend who, in need, complained of her delay in responding and "ghosted" her. So while I was not referring *directly* to the transference, I was attempting to use jointly formed alpha-elements from our analysis of the interaction with her friend and with me to give shape to the anxieties she was feeling now in relation to the manager. Despite appearance, I do not think of this as moving away from the *here and now* into the *there and then*, as in all three of these scenarios the *invariant* was a crisis with the love object that she felt she had wounded and possibly destroyed, and the persecutory guilt she was experiencing was present in the field here and now with me in the guise of the manager. This persecutory anxiety hampered her ability to represent the interaction realistically and had her on the brink of despair. My task, then, was to bring this specific anxiety, which found its way through each one of these relationships with minimal transformation, to the surface and lend my patient the words to think it, and in this way get a hold of what fear lay behind the compulsive reaction meant to vanquish it. I was concerned that Ms. C, who punished herself through depression or violence, would enter into a new phase of emotional self-devastation.

Here I think it is important for me to clarify what I mean by "compulsive reaction" meant to vanquish my patient's fear. As stated earlier, on the surface, Ms. C's behavior with her manager seemed to her to represent a reparative gesture, meant to atone for harm she acknowledged she committed against someone she loved. However, the harm in this case is imagined—the manager felt no such harm and only admitted to feeling disappointed mildly by Ms. C's having gone on vacation, and only when pressed to find the feeling inside of her specifically with respect to this. Ms. C then attached the manager's found feeling to being rushed out of the meeting. A partial reconstruction of her internal world at this point might connect whatever intolerable feelings were stirred in Ms. C for being rushed out of the room to her subsequent interpretation of her manager's ill motives, in the form of a projection, which then contributes to a T(+H) as I described earlier. In this way, an internal reality of harming or destroying the object becomes transformed into a hallucinosis of external reality. This is another way to make use of Bion's (1962b) concept of "reversible perspective", where the subject's experience of the outside coming in is the mirror image of what is inside coming out.

Indeed, Ms. C did offer "projection" as a possible way to understand the interaction but put this on the table in her familiar perfunctory way and rapidly dismissed it. I grasped at this opportunity to ask for her associations, and she immediately recalled having felt an overwhelming sense of envy earlier in the year when at another meeting, the manager was fawning over her colleague's pregnancy. We had discussed this then, and she now considered it analyzed and not related. I did not push. My patient could not feel angry at her beloved manager, who she instead felt was the one holding the anger, now directed toward her. Indeed, my patient would not accept her manager's explanation, suspecting that it existed in the latter's unconscious, which she could see. The obvious links between being rushed out and the manager's explanation were negatively hallucinated by Ms. C, transforming the act and the manager herself into bizarre objects that could not be understood outside of Ms. C's projected feelings of worthlessness and rage. The links between these elements of reality were attacked through negative hallucination to allow Ms. C to detach herself from her perception and evacuate the development of rage at an object she idealized. Thus, she could not feel her rage, only the persecution of the other.

It is important here to mention that this was the last of a series of events Ms. C brought up in the opening set of sessions following our break, which included most importantly a terrible argument with her father while away. The additional elements of her abrupt cancellation of two weeks of her analysis, the friend who she "left hanging", and now the harmed manager she worried was angry and retaliating at her, were all clearly linked together to one unconscious phantasy rudimentarily representing a mostly weakly represented experience of separation and object-loss. In the past, when Ms. C felt accused of doing something wrong, an accusation that never came explicitly but she interpreted whenever, for example, two or more people in her relational orbit came together without her, she often became enraged and lashed out violently against the primary offender or a proxy, usually her spouse. In this lashing out, the point was to "get into" the object the conviction that she was not as worthless as she was convinced she was being treated. She would make the other feel it, and the wish was to "leave them wordless", which in Bionese might be thought of as injecting the living "O" into them until they became the petri-fied, wordless embodiment of her own feelings of denigration. These states of rage would often last for days, more than once bringing her marriage dangerously close to an end and withering away her close friendships. Here we are talking about André Green's *passion*, as noted in the previous chapter, a kamikaze last-ditch attempt by the subject to generate a cognitive fabric through the force of emotion and action and stuff the void left behind by the de-cathexis of the object and the failure of representation—to do something, to place someone where there is noth-ing. Thus, Ms. C places the manager in the empty space of the unrepresented object and tries to restore her as a loving object through (manic) reparation that works more like reassurance of her self-worth.

Now, the patient, on return from her vacation, had begun telling me about her much-anticipated talk with her tyrannical and narcissistic father, almost a decade in the making and a subject of colossal ambivalence in her analysis. Her decade-long tentativeness about speaking with him had much to do with her aforementioned desire to find the exact words to leave him wordless, an impossible task not only for metapsychological or semantic reasons, but because she could already imagine, to the word, all of his impudent, arrogant counterresponses. Having merely informed me that she had finally had this long-anticipated conversation with her father, she suddenly dropped the subject, interrupting herself to move on to other more press-ing matters, mentioning only that it hadn't gone well. Most of the sessions during this week began in the same way, with her listing the possible topics she could talk about, the conversation being one of them, and then pressing on to other mat-ters without allowing space for reflection. Keeping in mind my patient's confusion about her and my vacation days, and our multiple related discussions, I began to feel that her continuous deferrals were not as much "resistance" as they were "tur-bulence" (Bion, 1965, p. 168), an inability to contain and transform within herself the powerful, painful, and confusing emotions this encounter with her father must have stimulated in her. In fact, the tentativeness I sensed in her about confirming our sessions prior to my vacation manifested itself in a similar way now with the topic of the conversation. I could sense in her anxiety about our session dates an invariance that connected us with her experience of her father, her friend, and her manager, each transformations of an O that was as yet unshareable.

But back to the manager. My previous interpretation about wanting to feel reas-sured that she was "good" came after 20 minutes of continuous speech from Ms. C where she ruminated about her manager. Without allowing the slightest space for reflection on what I said—this was not unusual for her, and we have tried to think about it in many unconvincing ways—Ms. C objected to the idea of having wanted to seem good and said she was interested only in letting her manager know she cared for her. She then pressed on, again without a moment for reflection, and continued to anxiously ruminate about her manager, to me an indication that her goal leaned more in the direction of protection from persecutory anxiety than of depressive reparation. She then told me that the previous day she had felt an enormous amount of anxiety about having been late to pick her young daughter up from school, fearing having caused her life-long emotional damage. And there was the friend who ghosted her after she was unable to return her call at exactly the time she was preoccupied with her child. Now she returned to the manager. Conscious of the likelihood of being stonewalled to the end, I stopped Ms. C and gently suggested that we should take a second to think about what she was telling me. I offered that she was feeling with her daughter and her friend the same as she felt with her manager, that she has irrevocably hurt someone and that something terrible will happen to her unless she finds a way to confirm that they are not angry with her and she is not bad. Ms. C responded that she didn't *feel* what I said was true, although it made sense, though each one of these situations was different. But what she wanted to communicate to me about the manager was more to do with having taken appropriate steps to make sure she understood that she cared. She then continued to speak without pause for many more minutes, going over the same material in loops, always landing where she was certain again about having *hurt* the manager by being away on vacation and wondering whether she could have been more explicit about her appreciation of her. She valued her relationship with her manager and would not want her manager to feel she had to stay away.

Weary of interrupting her again, I waited for her to take a breath to say I felt she was describing being afraid that her manager would end the relationship because she had determined despite her checking in with her that Ms. C was a *harmful* person she should stay away from, and that Ms. C wanted to show her otherwise and was worried she hadn't completed the job. Quite conscious of this being an extension of my earlier, rejected interpretation, I pressed on thinking it was worth the effort because it was worded more simply, and touched on the anxiety of her doubting whether she could have made her intentions more explicit to the manager, and the underlying conviction she herself felt of being a person worthy of scorn. Alas, this time Ms. C first asked me to explain my interpretation and then stopped me short of elaborating, asking me in a hurt tone why I had used the word "*harm-ful*". Taken aback at what seemed like being asked the obvious, and silently noting to myself that I was deferring registering her hurt tone, I said she had just finished telling me that she was worried that her manager would want to stay away to avoid feeling *hurt* by her. That implied, I added, that she thought the manager would find her "*harmful*" and want to stay away. Giving herself no space to think about my words, she responded that she didn't say that she had "harmed the manager", but that the manager might have felt "hurt" and conclude she didn't value their relationship. At this point, I found myself feeling that I had somehow told Ms. C that she had harmed/hurt the manager, an idea that was nowhere in what she had been saying. Moreover, I sensed that I myself had harmed her in making what now sounded like an accusation. An uncanny sensation of something unconscious becoming Reality came over me. In retrospect, I could see this as a transformation in O, where the unconscious context of the patient becomes the one Reality of the dyad. At the moment, however, I was mostly rattled, and circling back through our conversation in my mind, I found my thoughts in tangles. Had I been hallucinating? Was it "hurt", "harmed", "disappointed", all of the above or none of the above?

What were the *exact* words we used? Afterwards, I was able to see how the links between her words and statements uniting them in an emerging expression of an evolving, frightening idea of harming a loved object had been severed, or negatively hallucinated. In this way, it seemed to me, the harmed object became dis-objectalized, connecting no longer with my patient's subjectivity which was also negatively hallucinated in as much as her turbulent proto-emotions (what would have transformed into rage) had been evacuated, and the accusation of being a harmful person stopped being felt from the inside, coming now from me.

Interlude: the unbearable emptiness of transformations in hallucinosis

As I described in the previous chapters, transformations in negative hallucinosis has to do with all of the ways a subject unknowns their emotional experience by psychically disarticulating the elements that link this experience with common reality, transforming it in turn into an incomprehensible, yet lived-in other reality, which then begins operating by its own rules. This other reality becomes indistinguishable from anything other than a fact and can be lived-in but is ultimately not livable in any meaningful sense, as people may live long, hungry lives searching for a way out of something they are not aware that they are caught in. As another patient said to me, quoting the character Arthur Leander from *Station Eleven*, "I don't want to live the wrong life and die". A life that can be lived must first be dreamt, not hallucinated, as an individual "can get no more from a hallucination than he could get milk from an imaginary breast" (Bion, 1958–1979, p. 43). This hallucinated reality, as I have been describing in different ways, is what Bion refers to as O, which if the subject is unable to dream it, begins to persecute him as a lived experience of being and breathing-in the bad objects he is unable to metabolize and use as a source of knowledge about his feelings. In other words, only through dreaming can one transform O into K in a way that places limits and finitude on the infinity that is insufferable pain.

The reader at this point in the case narration might already have the sense of an evolving nightmare taking shape from which both participants are unable to awaken, what Ogden (2017) calls an "undreamt dream" and Cassorla (2018) calls a "non-dream-for-two". Much of the reason that it is so difficult for the analyst, who one thinks would know better, to step out of this type of enactment and reengage a capacity for dreaming the session (Bion, 1958–1979, p. 118; Ogden, ibid), is because of the tremendous pressure he feels by way of the patient's projective identification to *become* the evacuated beta-elements as a way of ensuring to the projector the success of the operation and the absence of the feelings inside of him. Additionally, perhaps paradoxically, the projector wants unconscious assurance that, being felt in his bones, the analyst has received his beta-elements as a communication, which can then be returned to the patient in a way that he will now be able to assimilate into his personality. But why would the patient want these beta-elements returned to them in the first place, even if coming back alphabetized?

This question is almost never asked in our literature, at least as far as I am aware of, but can be surmised if one digs deep into Klein's, Winnicott's, and Bion's writings where the nature of the infant's early ties with primary objects are essential to the constitutive experiences of the self. The proto-emotions, diffuse, unstructured, evanescent yet persistent, which drive these early interactions, are of primary importance in generating an internal sense of who the infant is and what the world is made of, and offer the first, and longest lasting link with reality, including whatever goodness there is to be had. Because of the aesthetic principle of the mind, emotions are the way the self discovers, creates, and knows the world. It is of upmost importance for the infant, and the infant within the evolving self, to maintain contact with its emotions if it is to maintain contact with life, as it is through emotions that the self can know and live in the world. Bion, as usual, is more succinct: "it is a short step from hatred of the emotions to hatred of life itself" (1958b, p. 150).

Ontological anxiety

Of course, the communication of these proto-emotions, or beta-elements, and their effective return to the patient is far from guaranteed. In having these experiences communicated to him in this way, that is, via projective identification, the analyst becomes transformed against his will. This transformation is not only produced in how he *thinks* of himself, i.e., "I am someone who hurts my patient", but also in how he *experiences* himself, "I am hurting my patient". There is a transformation from *having* a thought, to *being* a thought. And this transformation into being affects him at his essence, a transformation the analyst unconsciously and tenaciously resists. We are entering the territory of Chris Mawson's (2019) *ontological anxiety*, a kind of angst felt by the analyst when his inner sense of self is scrambled by the patient's unconscious role assignment. Mawson writes,

> We therefore need to consider the need for maintaining and furthering our capacity to being thrown by analytic listening, and by the forces of transference and countertransference, into estrangement from our everyday conceptions of our inner and outer worlds, including our current conceptions of psychoanalysis itself, since this too is not fixed . . . the analyst is at the focal point of having their sense of identity, their sense of being a particular person in a particular situation configured and reconfigured, and in the process, being "made-strange" in a manner outside their control. . . . This is an ontological anxiety at the heart of being an analyst—for periods of an analysis the transference processes create uncertainty and doubt over the question of who and what we are. Second, and consequent upon the first difficulty, we may feel anxiety at what we will visit upon our patient if, in the turbulent emotional storm created when two personalities meet we were to become, and enact upon the patient, one of the destructive objects or parts of the self in our own internal world.
>
> (Mawson, 2019, pp. 172–173)

I began to feel in the countertransference a sense that I had harmed and was harming Ms. C. But instead of taking a step back and reflecting on my role as the hurtful object, I felt compelled to move in the direction of wanting to make myself clear and pressing on. Only in retrospect was I able to recognize this as a case of my resisting ontological anxiety, related, as I will explain later, to what Bion (1958) called arrogance. Note, here I recognize being in the role of the harmful object but push aside the feelings, just as earlier I pushed aside my observation of a wounded tone in her response. These are all "thoughts without a thinker" requiring the analyst to capture them in order to move them from the countertransference and into reverie so as to dream them and place them back into the circulation of the field. T(−H), however, keep these thoughts from finding their thinker as the links between them and to the thinking-self become unseeable for fear of what emotion might materialize. The irony, of course, is that resistance to ontological anxiety impedes the movement into O, which would usher in a new experience that is transformative *because* it is catastrophic, and for that reason alone is feared and avoided. That is, the patient, in this case Ms. C, also feels ontological anxiety and has to defend against my interpretations that, for example, I am being experienced as her father so as to not consciously experience herself as her father's daughter outside of the defensive enclave she has built around herself. Here is Mawson again,

> Having introduced the strain for the analyst in taking the transference, which, as I say, includes not only the anxiety at being recruited into role relationships, and not only having painful feelings evoked, but also the ontological anxiety connected with the calling into question of who and what the analyst *is*, I now consider the difficulty due to an ominous sense in the analysis that an unwelcome discovery is about to happen. . . . In other words, the kind of resistance that I am considering is evoked when a patient or analyst begin to suffer the early stages of a premonition that an interpretation could precipitate a change from a familiar story to something real but as yet unknown. In my view, moments of threatened impingement into awareness of the real ($O \rightarrow K$) produce an additional level of insecurity, stemming from the ontological component (the awareness of mortality, or aloneness, for example), because there is no cure for the ontological, no "managing it", or "sorting-it-out", no reducing it through "knowing about it", only whatever may be mitigated by having someone with us in the experience, one who suffers with us the anxiety of the human condition.
>
> (Mawson, 2019, pp. 166–167)

In retrospect, the arrogance of pushing aside these feelings and persisting on making the same interpretation in variated forms was a sign that I was already engaged in a T(−H) with the patient, enacting an undreamt scene that, as we will see, portended her later account of what transpired with her father. Something unrepresented was transpiring between us, something on the level of "O" undergirding what on another level seemed like the rational discourse between analysand

and analyst trying to make themselves clear to each other. Something terrifying and in need of resisting because of what it made us to each other. But it is this catastrophe that has to be undergone and suffered, as to become O is to become the patient's internal world as it burns into the analyst. It is to allow the self to be transformed in a way that offers the dyad a canvas on which to bring to life the inner experiences of each, breaching the caesuras between inner and outer, self and object. This, of course, within the outer caesura of the frame constituted by the analyst's imperative to dream the session. Only in this way will painter and painted touch fingers.

Easier said than done when what is involved is the anguish of two people. Before the session ended, I was able only to register being stonewalled again and said I felt that she seemed to be splitting hairs with my words, as if she needed to protect herself from me, for fear of being criticized. She responded by saying that she didn't feel I was critical of her, but she felt I was pushy. I added "pushy like your father" to which she responded not being able to imagine my being like her father at all, as I was the exact opposite—caring, understanding, and receptive. I just had a way of pushing my views on to her that made her feel I was trying to take over her mind. "Like your father", I thought, but said nothing, and we left it there.

The following day, Ms. C said she had many "different" things to talk to me about but wanted to circle back to where we left off the day before. In her usual way she began searching her mind for the words we had exchanged and asked me what I meant by saying that she wanted to protect herself from me. I cautiously repeated a condensed version of what I said, weary of providing too many words to be contrasted against each other and dismissed. Now *I* was protecting myself from *her*. She responded with a familiar, "it makes sense, but I don't feel it". I had a sense, however, that Ms. C was *trying* to feel it, as if she could reach into her past and find an experience of her father to match her experience of me, whereas in my understanding, impossible to convey, the unconscious was present *right now*, in the conscious. There was no caesura between the two, and because her father and I had become concretized, she could not tell the two of us apart to be able to compare. The transference here had become a T(−H), stripped of any metaphoric qualities that would make me *like* the father, but rather a symbolic equation transference where I *was* the father. Since I was her father, Ms. C needed to tell me that she was not angry or upset with me, and that she loved me, all the while keeping a distance for fear that I would lash out.

Ms. C then said she wanted to "change the topic" and talk about what she *really* wanted to discuss, which was the long-awaited conversation. Ten years in the making, Ms. C had taken my suggestion and met with her father in a public place over dinner to limit his freedom to lash out at her violently. In this context, she too would have been restricted to expressing herself purely through words, which afforded her a feeling of safety against acting out. Nevertheless, the conversation got heated fast, and accusations flew. Her father rejected every single thing she said, insisting on his point of view, until only his verdict of her remained: she was selfish. This incredibly painful experience was very hard for her to talk about, and as she took the remainder of the session in describing it in painful detail, I thought of the ways in which that conversation seemed to virtualize our recent interaction, which in turn had concretized something that had seemed unrepresentable, until now. Might this only have become possible after Ms. C had a sense, through my enacting the pushy father, that her projective identifications had been received?

While I listened to Ms. C tell me about the conversation, I noticed in my mind images of the Cheshire Cat's smile, separated from the rest of its face,[2] and from the film *Snowden* that my patient and I had discussed seven years earlier. Back then, we had talked about a scene where Snowden's boss's face filled up the entirety of the wall screen in front of him. Both of these images, easily dismissible, became pictograms (Ferro, 2002), or ideograms (Bion, 1963), when I could think of them as instantly representing her father's mocking judgment, "You are Selfish!" as his face filled up the entirety of her subjectivity then and now. When the analyst is working in this way, he is working against the flow of T(−H), which would make nothing out of these linking products of the analyst's mind, and in the direction of alpha-functioning. I took a chance and said this painful conversation reminded me of *our* conversation the day before, where she felt that I was being pushy. Like at dinner with her father, I seemed to be taking up all the space. Alas, she responded that she had been planning on telling me about the dinner since before yesterday's session and did not see the connection. I felt thwarted, but optimistic. We ended for the week.

On Monday, Ms. C had many things she wanted to talk about but wanted first to circle back to our previous session the week before. She thought that our "argument" *did* in fact remind her very much of her argument with her father, but she still could not see me to be like him. I now noticed that it seemed as if she felt I was trying to convince her to feel I was like her father on a concrete level, not at all the intention of the transference interpretation of a moment in time where the patient seemed to be defending herself against an attack she perceived as coming from her analyst who at that moment was conflated with her father. There was a danger here, which I felt was familiar in our work when we both veered into intellectualization, in talking *about* a moment before having spent enough time thinking together from *within* it. This was always a problem when talking after the fact about something that occurred in a previous session, where the risk is of talking "about" rather than talking from *within* the transference, or as Mawson (2019) puts it, without "being informed". Mawson writes,

> Dwelling with being is best described not as knowledge about the patient, or insight into him, but of a becoming informed of his particular being in his worlds, inner and outer.
>
> (p. 123; my parentheses)

He goes on,

> This movement $(O \rightarrow K)$, in which intimations of "O" may become known from brief contacts with being (evolutions) I call becoming informed.
>
> (2019, p. 124)

"Being informed by being with", is Mawson's complete phrasing of it (ibid, p. 125). Ms. C wanted to know again what I meant, and I registered loudly and clearly an insistence in her voice that felt like a challenge. Feeling a lure to engage with her concretely, now at the level of answering questions, and of being enticed into an argument, I pulled back and waited. Ms. C said that if I *was* like her father, it was in that we were both pushy. She said she felt that I had been insisting too much on my point of view some sessions earlier when we were talking about her manager. That is why she contested the words I used to describe what she was feeling. I told her that I had indeed been pushy, and in that way, she was right to have to protect herself from me, for fear I might take over her mind, her words from one of those sessions. She then seemed confused and hurt, and asked me, "why would I want to protect myself from you? I don't think you are trying to hurt me". I sensed that something again had just happened inside my patient's mind that had made her bewildered. Where had the connections we had just made, *she* had just made, gone? Where had *she* gone? I began to feel the uncanny sensation of the patient hiding from me, as she hid from her father in childhood to avoid his wrath. Had my words to the effect that she was protecting herself from me felt like an accusation, as her father accused her of staying away from him? Was she telling me, her father, that she wasn't angry at me, lest we accuse her of being a bad daughter? In all of my transference interpretations about her wanting to keep a safe distance because she was afraid I would be angry and hurt her, had she been hearing me say to her, "don't run away from me, damn it, I am your father!" I held these thoughts in mind, as I considered what to say in a way that she could take in. I said, "I think you felt my words to be accusations". She took some time to think about this, again, something unusual in Ms. C, and came back with ". . . maybe. I don't know". She sounded disheartened.

Throughout the week, I found myself returning to our interactions and tried to understand where I was positioned in my patient's mind. Feeling deeply identified with a persecutory object, I could not see myself from without. I could not slip easily into the dream of the sessions and prepared before each as if for a fight. What would be the right words to say to her, to make her finally understand, I thought to myself, aware that she ruminated in the same manner about her father. What were the words I could say to myself, to best formulate for myself what was happening, the role I knew I was playing without knowing when and how I was playing it? How did I continue to make Ms. C feel the need to protect herself from me, with every word I said, every thought I attempted to translate into words, possibly with my tone, most likely with my insistences, and to cause her to split my words, her thoughts, and in so doing, expand the universe of her and my anxiety? My insistences *did not feel that way* in the moment they were uttered, and rather felt like answers to her questions, a few words I managed to get in through a break in the wall of words she erected between us. To me they made sense within the contexts of what we were talking about, and related directly to how I was feeling in the moment with the patient, be it protective, attacked, criticized, neutralized. Yet my words *did* feel that way after saying them, when they became constantly conjoined with her responses. Her protectiveness seemed to precede my interpretations yet were also a reaction to them. Causality was lost, all attempts to pull things together futile. By the end of the week, I began experiencing myself as an analyst who harmed my patient, who criticized her, pointed out things that she didn't want to see about herself, and made her feel she was hiding things from me. I did not like the feeling.

On arrogance

I am tempted here to refer to myself in the third person when saying that the analyst in the previous description of Ms. C's analysis was acting under the sway of *arrogance*, which Bion says is a trait of the clinician who, like Oedipus, does not heed Tiresias' warning about the reckless pursuit of truth. With Ms. C, the chronic enactment enabled by the T(−H) of the connections in our minds that would have allowed us to see how we were concretizing through action the unprocessed, unformulated, re-traumatizing experience with her father, defended against the entry of this shared O into the dream, out of the anxiety of being at-one-with the experience of being the abusive father abusing the abused daughter. The T(−H) abets the analyst, though we should say the dyad because there are two of us exerting pressure in this experience, in resisting the ontological anxiety of becoming O, of having the emotions emerge with both consciousnesses there to receive them in all their unpleasantness. Allowing for the unpleasant feelings to emerge from their proto-emotional, amorphous state, now in the structuring relation of an object relationship, involves accepting the patient's projective identifications, a first step of which is recognizing them for what they are. The threat of guilt induced by these projective identifications mobilizes the analyst to get rid of them fast, and he does so by setting out in search of the cause and culprit, which unbeknownst to himself is him. The analyst in this way refuses the patient's projective identifications, which he experiences as things-in-themselves, and does not realize that the patient is communicating *in the language* of projective identification. This has to do with Bion's theory of functions, where the analyst must consider that his anxiety is letting him know that there is something he is not understanding. The anxiety itself must be dreamt as a projective identification of the analyst to himself in the form of a communication, and not a persecutory feeling. In this way, the analyst's ear is turned toward his emotions in relation to the patient and can dream them now as communications rather than merely evacuative attacks.

I mentioned Oedipus because this is the character that Bion has the analyst play in his short paper where he does not talk specifically about T(H), but instead develops ideas that will be furthered in his next paper, *Attacks on Linking* (1958b), which formulate the psychic processes of anti-linking that I've described make up T(H) and by implication, T(−H). But Oedipus is also the patient in the sense that Bion is describing the functioning of the psychotic part of the mind that is present in all of us at determined moments. And so, Ms. C can also not afford to allow herself to experience the O of the session, as this too confronts her with the ontological anxiety of dreaming and be-coming the undreamt enraged girl now in relation to the analyst-father. She too must turn a blind eye, upholding the fantasy of an ideal (analytic) family as a defense against the trauma of her real family (Steiner, 2018). As we can see, then, Bion's reading of the Oedipus myth underscores a different set of psychic and human calamities than illustrated in Freud's well-known narrative around the incestuous and murderous relationship of Oedipus to King Laius and Jocasta. Freud reads the Oedipus story as illustrating the psychic content of maturation and sexual development, while Bion emphasizes the components that illustrate the development of the *apparatus for thinking* thoughts.[3] For Bion, then, this is a story that has at its crossroads the question of *knowing* (K, or curiosity) versus *not-knowing* (negative capability). In its extremes, Oedipus' curiosity represents the former and Teiresias' admonishment against his investigations into the cause of the plague that befell Thebes the latter. For Bion, there is a warning here about the overzealous pursuit of truth at any costs, without adequate attention to the patient's defenses and modes of communication. Paradoxically, the pursuit of truth may become a form of evading reality; like Schliemann's excavations of Troy, the analyst-archaeologist effaces the very thing he seeks to unearth.

In *On Arrogance* (1958a), Bion lays out what he feels is at the basis of the psychological catastrophe of patients such as Ms. C who construct psychic fortifications against relational trauma. Signs that a psychological catastrophe has indeed occurred are dispersed throughout a patient's presentation and are usually in the form of what Bion refers to as the scattered presence of *Curiosity*, *Stupidity*, and *Arrogance*. These three belated and traumatized prophets, survivors of an ancient shipwreck, wander in and out of the session, unknown to each other, until the analyst, through repetition, gets a sense of their interfamilial ties and begins to realize that not far behind lie the ruins of a psychological trauma. Perhaps *curiosity* doesn't feel too malignant a word, but *stupidity* and *arrogance* carry strong connotations that I think have to do with what Bion felt to be an urgent clinical situation.[4] We understand that Bion is not only describing the patient's psychological disaster in these terms, but just as importantly, the analyst's. *Curiosity* is the desire for truth. Oedipus wants to know. The patient wants to know who they are and who their analyst is—curiosity, yet they also do *not* want to know, and want to be ignorant of the therapist's reality—stupidity. According to Bion, truth is to the mind what food is to the body—curiosity for truth—but the mind cannot symbolize, represent all it encounters, much of reality being ineffable when not traumatic—stupidity. The patient and analyst enter this joint pursuit of knowledge called psychoanalysis with enough arrogance to imagine themselves unscathed in the process.

Stupidity here is a word that merits further qualification. Bearing in mind what I just mentioned about how these harsh terms reflect for Bion the stark realities of the emotional catastrophe that arrogance, stupidity, and curiosity portend, we can say the analyst is stupid in an arrogant way not when he is able to suspend memory and desire and in that way "not know", but when he is *unable* to do the same and therefore lives in a state of persecutory stupidity, which he tries to undo by knowing precipitously or prematurely. Likewise, the patient too is stupid when defending himself against this type of analyst by making himself numb to the person he is to become and keeping himself from inhabiting his undreamt life. The patient may be wise to remain stupid, as he is protecting himself after all from an overly-curious and anxious analyst, but he is nevertheless resisting an experience that for better or for worse points to an underlying O of the dyad, one that, owing to the analyst's own stupidity, arrogance, and curiosity, has yet to become a shareable and livable O. At a deeper level, the patient understands he will not learn from experience but instead will be retraumatized.

For instance, Ms. C often fell asleep in sessions, almost always without fail when I began speaking. At times the falling asleep seemed to me to be a type of digestive slumber owing to too much interpretative content on my part, even though often it seemed as if no amount of modulation or modification of my words, including shortening sentences or simplifying, prevented her from slipping into a dreamless sleep. Ms. C carried out a T(−H) of her own when in response to my gentle probing of her sudden sleepiness, she tended to state that she literally had just had a meal, which carried for her the conviction of reality since our sessions were usually in the morning or around noon. My sense after a while was that my calling attention to this made her feel persecuted, and I interpreted this, eliciting in response the exact opposite from my patient: perhaps it was that the sound of my voice was so soothing, she could not resist falling asleep. I was meant to feel that my words were of secondary, if any, importance, as I had helped her by incarnating the good object in session, and that was enough. For my part, this left me feeling disarmed, a feeling which arose après-coup, leading me to sense that something potentially dangerous was being avoided by the patient in ignoring my words and going to sleep. Post-slumber she often asked if I could repeat, the emotional moment having passed, the connection weak when not impotent or futile. My words were unavoidably confusing since they no longer referred to something alive moments earlier but had gone away, hidden, in the sleep.

Only experience taught me that repeating my interpretation at the patient's request post-slumber and post-mortem enacted a reckless barreling down deeper (arrogance) into the earth in pursuit of a patient who had gone underground and, in doing so, damaged layer upon layer of important emotional texture that the both of us could otherwise see. Curiosity is again what's at stake here. As mentioned earlier, out of the three, curiosity is the most benign sounding of the survivors of the primitive catastrophe, in part due to the fact that it is linked with the epistemophilic instinct and the desire for Truth, and therefore a natural component of the psychoanalytic function of the mind. What we are talking about then is curiosity linked with the death drive, as a desire to know borne out of tension reduction in the subject that ultimately enacts a T(−H), which mystifies more than discovers. The knowledge that is gained from this type of curiosity unleashed is a form of -K, producing a form of certainty in both patient and analyst—mainly analyst—who doggedly pursues more and more evidence which he then finds in the patient's resistance. Prideful in his interpretation—after all Bion tells us that pride linked with the death drive is what arrogance is (Civitarese, 2021, p. 237)—the analyst's curiosity "mirrors the curiosity that produced the catastrophe of the psychosis. It is in itself a form of 'psychosis'. The analyst's obstinate curiosity to know reinforces the patient's resistance to not want to know and induces further regression" (Ibid, p. 242).

One of the important lessons from *On Arrogance*, then, is Bion's advice to the analyst to listen to the patient's mode of communication more than to her words, although this too must be qualified. Ms. C may have been right by implying that it didn't matter what I said so long as I was a soothing presence to her, if what she was communicating was that the medium is the message, as Marshall McLuhan famously said, and that the meaning of the words, if they are to have any, has to be heard in the patient's methods of communicating and in the experience of being communicated to in a particular way. That is, for Bion, the analyst thinks he is speaking with a patient who is using language as a mode of communication and does not realize the extent to which projective identification is influencing what is being communicated. The analyst often is unaware of the extent to which they themselves "cannot stand" this mode of communication. Bion writes about his patient, who in a session talked about "an obstructive force", which he later identified with Bion, someone he felt "could not stand it":

> What it was that the object could not stand became clearer in some sessions where it appeared that in so far as I, as analyst, was insisting on verbal communication as a method of making the patient's problems explicit, I was felt to be directly attacking the patient's methods of communication. From this it became clear that when I was identified with the obstructive force, what I could not stand was the patient's methods of communication. In this phase my employment of verbal communication was felt by the patient to be a mutilating attack on his methods of communication. From this point onwards, it was only a matter of time to demonstrate that the patient's link with me was his ability to employ the mechanism of projective identification. That is to say, his relationship with me and his ability to profit by the association lay in the opportunity to split off parts of his psyche and project them into me.
>
> (Bion, 1958a, p. 146)

So we hear Bion as Tiresias warning us that the reckless pursuit of the truth, without an appreciation for the ego's capacity to metabolize it, what he calls arrogance, can add to the psychological disaster the therapist seeks to get to the bottom of. As her analyst and Oedipus, I wanted to end the dreadful plague of alienation from others that Ms. C had been suffering from for most of her life. This was not my conscious pursuit, but I recognized it over time as an unconscious phantasy that could upend my analytic listening, close to Freud's warning to Ferenczi about his furor sanandi (Freud, 1915, p. 171). In a mirror way, Ms. C wanted to end the plague of cold and hostile distance existing between herself and her father and planned endlessly for a final conversation that would put the matter to rest, leaving him with an overwhelming sense of remorse, regret, guilt, and desire to repair their relationship. But this wish of Ms. C's took no consideration of her father's point of view, and being the tyrant that he often was, his point of view was unthinkable outside of his propensity for violence. This is part of the tragedy, where Oedipus Rex turns into Oedipus Tyranus, and the tyrants in both Ms. C and her father seek to communicate through projective identification with neither of them being able to assume the roles of container. So Bion reminds us that Oedipus' pursuit of the truth, no matter how much it benefited the city of Thebes in stopping the plague, led to his destructive self-attacks, exile, and the suicide of Jocasta, not to the reparation he and my patient desired. Similarly, the analyst's pursuit of verbal interpretation when containment of the patient's projective identification is warranted can lead to negative therapeutic reactions in the patient who cannot psychologically process the truth. So for Bion the "arrogance" of the analyst is when he expects that the patient will communicate in the analyst's preferred mode of communication, i.e., words that convey meaning, rather than what the patient has available to her. Here we see Bion's extension of Melanie Klein's use of projective identification as *a mode of communication* and not merely as *evacuation*, a form of the defense he terms *realistic* or *normal* projective identification (Bion, 1958b, 1962a). Indeed, as stated earlier, the patient both *evacuates* intolerable emotions into the analyst as a way of getting assistance with them, as well as *communicates* to him the nature of these emotions. In this way, the projected content is less semantic and can be theorized as "force without ideational content" (Levine, 2022, p. 22), unrepresented states that have to do more with *experiences* of the patient that have not been successfully processed and remain in the realm of procedural memory linked to certain intersubjective dilemmas, such as to trust or not to trust, to connect or not to connect, to leave her state of slumber or to go underground again.

Keeping in mind that for the moment, Ms. C's preferred mode of communication is projective identification, I am no longer (as) *stupid* to this. My task now is to not obstruct her communication and to avoid installing myself as a projective identification denying superego, one that deprives her of even this mode of linking to me by destroying her ability to think even further. It seems strange to consider projective identification and thinking as intricate to each other, because of the former's evacuative function, but Bion explains that it is in the "sojourn in (the analyst's) psyche" (Bion, 1958a, p. 146) that the ability to use an object for verbal communication depends. Only then can actual thinking happen. When under this strain the analyst is able to remain in a state of *negative capability*, which we might now think of as a *negative* form of *curiosity* linked with the life drive, he makes room for anxious uncertainty to be transformed through an act of faith into something that will evolve if the analyst allows it (Bion, 1970, p. 255). This act of faith, borne through negative capability, may also help the analyst stay in his seat when the patient becomes attacking, accusatory, or rejecting, all situations that can test even the seasoned analyst's sense of professional and personal pride. For Bion, pride in the service of the life drive is *self-respect*, whereas linked with the death drive, as I mentioned earlier, it becomes *arrogance* (Civitarese, 2021, p. 237).

Bion, of course, was not naïve. He understood that psychoanalysis was itself part of the problem. As he puts it, "Unfortunately, the problem is complicated by a fact which must already be evident—the analytic procedure in itself is already a manifestation of the curiosity which is felt to be an intrinsic component of the disaster" (1958, p. 132). This is an important note to highlight in this paper written early in his career, but included in his later *Second Thoughts* (1967) compiled on the cusp of his more thorough examination of O in *Attention and Interpretation* (1970), and containing the genesis of his theories of alpha-functioning and container ↔ contained, which will later appear there. Patient and analyst enter an analysis together because both are curious about emotions and seek to have contact with them, especially painful ones that they do not yet have the capacity to contain. This is one pillar of the catastrophe that befalls the analytic couple and perhaps all of us as human beings when we seek to find ourselves in our relations with the other, whose otherness we have not fathomed and cannot fathom from previous experience. "As a consequence," Bion writes, "the very act of analyzing the patient makes the analyst an accessory to precipitating regression and turning the analysis into a piece of acting-out" (idem).

So what is there to do? Bion here advises us to embrace this curiosity in a way that would foster humility rather than fuel the fires of arrogance, and in doing so, to "make the best out of a bad job" (Bion, 1976–1979, p. 136). He writes,

> From the point of view of successful analysis, this is a development that should be avoided. Yet I have not been able to see how this can be done. The alternative course is to accept the acting out and the regression as inevitable, and if possible to turn it to good account.
>
> (1958a, p. 132)

Bion next advises the analyst to stay as close as possible to the present moment with the patient, second by second, moment to moment, and construct "a detailed interpretation of events that are taking place in the session" (idem). The analyst must always perform in this sense the opposite of arrogance and assume that at every moment he is part of the crime that he is investigating. He therefore must remain vigilant of not "turning a blind eye", as in Steiner's use of the term, to the fact that stupidity will follow him and the patient every step of the way, when stupidity refers to the expected failure of the analytic couple to link up with each other's preferred method of communication.

Returning to our conversation[5]

Ms. C and I found ourselves once again at an impasse at the end of the last session. I was left with a pervading feeling that our words and the conclusions we could draw from them had become excessively concrete. This filled me with the disconcerting feeling that I was again doing to my patient something that was causing her pain, a feeling that only in retrospect I would understand as signaling the emergence of a shareable O. At the moment, however, it was arousing intense onto-logical anxiety in me.

Rather than being able to think about this feeling using binocular vision (Bion, 1965, p. 185), that is, from multiple vantage points that I could then share with Ms. C, I felt a burgeoning sense, I think in her as well as in me, that our interaction was denuded of meaning and becoming a thing-in-itself, a T(−H). As I listened to her, my mind went everywhere and nowhere. On the one hand, I tried to concentrate on her exact words and back-track, to see where I had gone adrift. This is what Bion referred to as searching for causality, trying to restore a sense of logical space and time, the kind that someone who is lost might understandably grasp at, but that is of a radically different nature from unconscious experience (1967, p. 199).

However, another part of my mind kept moving toward other directions. Over the course of the week and in between sessions, I began noticing intrusive thoughts, including memories from my own summer break where, having had a flat tire on a far-flung country road in a foreign land, I had to decipher the instructions of our rental's tire foam compressor kit after discovering there was no spare in the trunk. Written in a foreign language on a multi-page manual replete with arrows, sym-bols, and minuscule font, the situation was as near to catastrophic as I could man-age while on vacation. Returning now as reverie, I could view these two apparently separate trains of thought as the convergence of crucial lines of communication within the bidirectional flow of the field. The flat-tire memories, in constant con-junction with my compulsion to solve the crime of who said what and when in the session, began to make sense to me as my way of representing how I was trying to speak to my patient in a language that was foreign to her. Conversely, I was hearing her in a language that was foreign to me and enforcing a manualized interpreta-tion that required us to go by the rules of reality and common sense. Reality and common sense, to me anyway, required that there be a spare tire in the trunk of the rental. I did not expect to see the empty space where instead of a spare, there was a compressor kit. This may seem like a glib thought to have, but it was the shock of the moment that kept coming back to me in fragments that, gathered together, I could begin to think of as my reverie. Further thoughts led me to wonder if I was using my interpretations as a sort of foam that would fill up a tear of unrepresent-ability that I and Ms. C were coming up against in her psyche. Dreaming these frag-ments of my reverie, I could now more easily feel how the flat-tire concreteness that characterized our various impasses was connected to my attempts at pushing for representations based on foam, rather than a more connected experience of the O of the session. It was at these moments that Ms. C abruptly became confused, fell asleep, or forgot what we had just been talking about.[6]

Ms. C began this session now with her wanting to return to the conversation from the session before, which occurred on the last day of that week. I had sug-gested to her again that she felt she needed to protect herself from me, lest I make her feel I would take over her mind with my pushiness. This made sense to her, but she could not *feel* it, an experience she often reported and that I had grown to con-sider was a way of her keeping the meaning and implications of the interpretation at bay. She again spoke about the importance of our relationship, an importance that I did not doubt, but that nevertheless reminded me of the stakes involved in her coming to terms with anything less than loving feelings for an equally loving analyst father. She stressed how desperate the whole conversation with her father had made her feel, and how he blamed her for everything, and I silently noted what I had begun thinking earlier, that she took my interpretations as blaming her for having the "wrong feelings", the same way her father did. The next day, Ms. C told me about how she "set limits" with her friend who had "ghosted" her, and then about her father's accusations to her that she had selfishly "disappeared" on him. This thought enraged her and instantly brought to her mind the memory of the meeting where her manager gushed over her colleague's pregnancy. Her father too would like to spend more time with others than with her, but she is not picking up the phone when he calls. I said,

> your father and his friends, your manager and your pregnant colleague, all of these come together with the feeling that they are separate from you. They harm you when they are with others, it's like they leave you and go away. You don't want to let them back in, they are like ghosts to you. But you also love them, you don't want to ghost them completely.

Ms. C responded by saying that she could "understand" where I was coming from, but she did not *feel angry* at her manager. She then doubted whether there was much of a connection between the situations I was describing and asked me to explain what I meant. I said that maybe "understanding" what I meant but then not seeing a connection was a way of protecting herself from feeling angry. She responded by saying, almost self-mockingly, but in a way that made me feel again that I had said something wrong, "of course, Psych 101!"

The following day, Ms. C was distraught. Upon leaving our session, she came home to find her husband and daughter taking selfies together. This stung and angered her, stirring up old familiar feelings of painful exclusion by others. Having recognized her feelings for what they were, she managed to the extent that she could and went on with her day. In the morning, however, before our session, Ms. C walked into the kitchen to find the two of them having breakfast. Not registering what she was feeling at the moment, she opened the refrigerator to find that the bottle of milk she had expected to reach for was not there. Now she turned to see her husband and daughter drinking from it and erupted in a rage. She lost control of herself and screamed at the two for being inconsiderate of her and of not appreciating everything that she did for them. An all-too-common situation unfolded that left everyone, including Ms. C, traumatized and in tears.

We talked about the back and forth of her thinking before her explosion and eventually reached a point where I said to her that she was feeling left out of the selfie-picture in the same way she felt left out of her father's life and out of my life, when she felt that I don't see her in my interpretations, only reflections of myself. I added that this made her feel that she was not being considered by me or others and that she and her feelings were worthless to us. She agreed and said that she felt like a character in the TV show *Futurama*, who often says his time can't be wasted because it is worthless. She is never taken into consideration anywhere she goes, and all I seemed to offer was that she must just learn to put up with it. I then reminded her that at the end of our last session, she made a self-deprecating comment about "Psych 101" that made me think that she might have felt that I had treated her like she was stupid, by suggesting that she was protecting herself against anger by understanding and then taking apart the connections between the words that I said. She responded that if she didn't now agree with *this* interpretation, I would accuse her again of protecting herself, so she didn't know what to do. I said we were at the dinner table, and she felt she had no way out but to agree with me. I added that my using the words "protecting herself" implied to her that I felt she was doing something wrong, which made her feel trapped. If she disagreed, she was being oppositional, just like her father accused her of being. Ms. C took this in an said this made her think that the previous week, I hadn't taken her into consideration when she insisted that she was not trying to show her manager that she wasn't a "bad person", but that she wanted to show the manager that her feelings were important to her. I said that like in *Futurama*, I had made her feel her thoughts were worthless. Astounded, I then heard her ask me *what, if anything, did this have to do with how she felt that morning with her husband and daughter*. Taking note of the moment, which I understood as a response to my *Futurama* interpretation and having to do with the O of the session where the bottom seems to drop out in Ms. C's emotional experience, I said that I felt we were trying to pull something together that was happening now between the both of us, where she was telling me that she felt hurt and disregarded by me—the way she felt with her husband and daughter, who she also felt were *selfishly* taking all of the milk and leaving her with nothing (the missing spare tire in the rental car). I suggested that this infuriated her but prior to that left her feeling extremely confused, not understanding what had happened. Why was she excluded? Why was the milk missing? Where was she in her husband's and her daughter's minds? I said that in a fit of (Greenian) passion, she railed against the two of them as if to say she existed and to burn that living existence into them as a guarantee that she was not worthless and would not be ignored. If she did not do this, she felt she would be letting herself disappear, becoming more and more depressed, until finally becoming a ghost of herself altogether. My sense is that with passion, Ms. C forces the fading preconception of her own subjectivity into a confrontation with the Real of raw emotion, as if attempting to materialize a container through which to feel her existence, as if to realize an encounter with an object that never arrived. I have not gone into the details here of Ms. C's early life history in respect of her privacy, but suffice to say there was severe early deprivation. The last thing I mentioned in my interpretation to Ms. C, which was slow and in parts, and in the form of a dialogue rather than of a father pushing assertions on her from across the dinner table, was that when I told her that she was concerned about being seen as "bad" to her manager, and overlooked her concern for her manager's well-being, she heard me telling her that she only thought of herself and was therefore selfish.

Postscript. When representations fail

What happened inside of Ms. C when she opened the refrigerator to find that the bottle of milk was *missing*? What turbulence moved inside of her when she observed her husband and daughter taking selfies *without* her, and then the next day, having breakfast *in her absence*? How does this all lead to the buildup and then violent explosion that occurs as a result? To understand this, a small detour and a deeper dive is necessary into the meaning of the psychoanalytic term "representation", a concept that has been used ubiquitously throughout this text, to say nothing of our literature, most of the time taking for granted the reader's knowledge. Throughout this book, I have been emphasizing how the process of T(−H) involves a deactivation of cathected representations, that is, of un-representing, followed by the disabling of the ability to represent altogether, leading to a barren, concrete "as-is" (not the same as "as-if") situation that persecutes the subject (because it cannot be processed through meaning) and presents him with ultimate Reality, O, ineffable, irreducible experience that cannot be grasped through multiple vertices, and only experienced as excess. The experience is sublime, and as such un-sublimated. Likely, however, we are dealing with different *degrees* of representation, or localized and contextualized loss of complete representation. But the psychanalytic term "representation", which of course originates in Freud, has a long history which I will not go into here. Instead, I will only touch upon where it stands in the contemporary literature within the framework of Greenian, Bionian, and post-Bionian psychoanalysis.

If it began as a relatively simple term, used interchangeably with psychic representation, mnemic trace, and mental image, and denoted simply "the relatively permanent image" of something that has been previously perceived (Rycroft, 1995, p. 157), at this point in our history the concept has become much more sophisticated. Interestingly, "representation" does not appear in the authoritative Laplanche and Pontalis (1973) dictionary, although the term "considerations of representability" does appear (p. 389). Laplanche and Pontalis write that these considerations of representability are the requirement imposed on dream-thoughts, which undergoing transformation give them the capacity to be "represented" by images, particularly visual images. Here we are already talking about the ability of the mind to form "thoughts" that can be visualized, that is, held in mind apart from the internal or external object of experience. The degree to which these "visual" thoughts take on meaning marks the extent to which they become "ideas". Micro transformations happen along the way, and perhaps the best way to think of the total process, as I suggested earlier, is one of degrees of representability rather than representation one and all. That is, at least until the mind has reached a level of maturity where the act of representation has been internalized as a function. Howard Levine (2022) is clear on this matter:

It is important to emphasize that references to representational "weakness" or absence do not necessarily imply a complete lack of "registration" or "inscription" in the psyche or soma, but instead different levels or gradients or inscriptions, with representation being among the most highly organized and advanced.

(pp. 20–21)

At a basic level, then, "representation refers to the psychic capacity to keep present, in one's mind, what is not in one's perceptual field" (Sparer, 2010, p. 1182). Of course, Laplanche and Pontalis do refer in their *Language of Psychoanalysis* to word-presentation and thing presentation, the basic elements of Freud's theory of representation and memory, and it is within this framework that representation is understood within a functioning, neurotically organized mind. Thus, Levine (2022) defines representation as

organized, structured psychic entities that are potentially verbalizable as thoughts, ideas or images. Representations can be invested with emotions, linked together into narratives and, if put into suitable form [the unification of word presentations and thing presentations (Freud, 1915)], they may be eligible to pass censorship and enter consciousness.

(p. 3)

However, when an individual's mind is lacking the structure that makes representation possible, that structure in itself accrued through a history of successful-enough experiences with representation, difficulties follow where

the patient can only "think" when the object is present in external reality. In the absence of the object, such patients remain action-bound, rather than being capable of emotionally invested thought. Patients who cannot effectively think or imagine have no other recourse than acting out or somatic discharge.

(Levine, 2013, p. 47)

Whatever regulatory function representation had achieved cedes to passion. The ability to link elements together into a discursive sequence constituting conscious and unconscious thinking gives way, and the drives—those elements in need of representation—not only become bound to an external trigger but pose an internal problem.

The internalization of the function of representation over time has become one of the aims of psychoanalytic treatment. Writing on this topic in relation to the work of André Green, Levine writes that

Green noted that Freud's theoretical shift marked a change from a theory centered upon psychic contents (ideational *representations*) to a theory about the movements needed to tame the unstructured, not yet represented aspects of *the drive*—that is, emotion, impulse, and somatic discharge—within the psychic apparatus. Thus, the aim of analytic treatment shifted to: "Where Id was, there Ego shall be", with the important proviso that the drive was now not only a problem for the ego, but a problem *within* the ego.

(Levine, 2023, pp. 2–3; italics in the original)

When a robust representational function has not been internalized, the subject is prone to passion, one of the three modalities of affect, including emotion and feeling that Green (1999a) outlines, and the one with the most devastating consequences on the psyche if for its essential unruliness. Green writes

The affect appears to be taking the place of representation. The process of linkage is a linkage of cathexes in which the affect has an ambiguous structure. In so far as it appears as an element of discourse, it is subjected to that chain, includes itself in it as it attaches itself to the other elements of discourse. But insofar as it breaks with representations, it is the element of discourse that refuses to let itself be linked by representation and takes its place. A certain quantity of attacked cathexis is accompanied by a qualitative mutation; the affect may then snap the chain of discourse, which then sinks into non-discursivity, the unsayable. The affect is then identified with the torrential cathexis that breaks down the dikes of repression, submerges the abilities of linkage and self-control. It becomes a deaf and blind passion, but ruinous for the psychical organisation.

(p. 283)

Passion rushes in to replace a representation that is missing, which would contain an irreplaceable object. Green relates passion to interminable mourning (p. 284), and in this way we may conceive of this irreplaceable object not only as the lost object of melancholia, but as the object that is at once irreplaceable and unlocatable in the psyche, the primary object and all the related experiences in early development that encompass it, and through which the subject learns from experience to self-regulate. The absence of this object leaves such a hard inscription in the psyche that it tears it, a tear in the fabric of the psyche (Green, 2005).

This brings us to the basic situation that Bion (1962b) termed learning from experience. To represent emotion is to experience it, and once experienced it can be experienced again, with less need for distancing the self from it, as it becomes gradually more tolerable and internalized. This may seem too simple a situation, and perhaps it is, but it requires a consciousness expanded and enhanced by words when they become available, and immersed in experiences with objects that serve as containers before the eventual advent of language. None of this is a forgone conclusion, in particular in early preverbal infancy where, according to Bion, the psyche is at a crossroads every time it encounters a new emotion. Each time, it makes a choice between evading the emotion or modifying it. Evasion leads to processes on the continuum of the negative, ending in T(−H), while modification is what we do when we make emotion more tolerable by forming an abstracted version of it in our minds, a representation, and internalizing it. And importantly, as I mentioned earlier, to internalize is to transform the act of representation into an unconscious function of the ego, a function that is exercised by what is now a good internal object, that is, a place within oneself from which one can hold and regard emotional experience. In the same way that the parent's care of their child is transformed into the child's ability to take care of themselves without having to consciously think of the parent, the subject meets previously emotionally difficult situations with more equanimity and familiarity, without the need for a defensive overreaction. They have represented and internalized the external object, which has now been transformed into a function. This, I think, is what Bion meant by "learning". For instance, Ms. C would arrive at a place where she knows that when she is excluded she feels worthless, but she is able to allow this feeling to exist within herself as one of many ways she feels about herself, without it *becoming* her, i.e., without it becoming the Only convincing way she feels about herself, or Ultimate Reality, and without the subsequent need to passionately lash out for recognition. She would represent the feeling and experience it as such—an emotional experience within herself and not a sign of the other's intentions or feelings—staying connected to, while maintaining a thinkable distance from the turbulence inside. This new vantage point would offer her potential space to include fuller representations of the other two people in the room, and in creating this space within herself, indeed the act of representing itself, she is modifying her internal experience and regulating her emotional response. Representation now becomes a function, and thinking can occur in the absence of a good external object otherwise necessary to block out the hostile, internal presence of the nothing.

The regulatory functions of representations that have done their job, in healthy development and a good analysis transform emotions, then, into inner structure (good internal objects), which holds an individual through difficult moments. These functions, however, are always susceptible to breakdown in extreme circumstances. For instance, in moments of absolute helplessness that signal the threat of utter "breakdown", this function may not always be counted on, as Bion was alluding to when noting that dying men on the battlefield call out for their mothers, as Sweeting did in his final moments as recounted in Chapter 1. We may imagine that men and women in a state of dementia are experiencing something similar when also calling out for their mothers, an experience of something terribly, irrevocably, and enigmatically gone wrong inside and the need for a mother to contain it. The preconception remains operative—the individual calls for "mother"—but in the case of dementia, actual time would have to be reversed to early infancy for a realization to transform into a conception. The preconception remains empty, the call perpetually unanswered, and it is striking how often these individuals cry out that they have been abandoned by a mother they have no memory of. The breakdown has occurred.

In moments when the self feels *on the brink* of utter breakdown, the conceptions that have been laid down by experience may falter. Bion writes that

> Normal development follows if the relationship between infant and breast permits the infant to project a feeling, say, that it is dying into the mother and to reintroject it after its sojourn in the breast has made it tolerable to the infant psyche. If the projection is not accepted by the mother the infant feels that its feeling that it is dying is stripped of such meaning that it has. It therefore reintrojects, not a fear of dying made tolerable, but a nameless dread.
>
> (Bion, 1962a, p. 183)

In absence of the real thing, one has no recourse but to cry out to the primary object, to the mother, to try and transform the faltering representation, the word and thought "mother", into a realization—to make the fading representation/conception real—that would merge with the anguish of dying that has become one's entire being, in order to transform this fear of dying into a tolerable fear. One tries to return to an "O" of at-one-ment, in order to slow down and steady the "O" of unbearable infinity that, in the moment of death, is meant to be taken in. I think that when Ms. C opened the refrigerator, she was already in a state where she was searching for the realization of a containing breast (the bottle of milk) that would counterbalance the pull toward the negative of evacuating emotions into a state of T(−H) where her experience of becoming dead inside would grow denser and the ghost become stronger. When, upon opening the refrigerator, the existence of the "missing bottle of milk" was what was "realized", instead of encountering the representation "no-milk" she experienced "nothing", the tear in the fabric of the psyche through which her subjective sense of being would dissolve if not for ruinous passion. Perhaps *passion*, then, in its doomed attempt to plug the hole (Reed & Baudry, 2005), becomes a way of trying to awaken the subject from the transformation in negative hallucinosis that has held it in its grip, and through becoming the Real of experience defying all representation, attempts to provoke, stimulate, and electrify a container into existence.

Notes

1 Here, I would like to introduce the specifications for what I mean by "affects", used throughout the chapters in this book as a general term, but in this chapter a term that needs to be placed in relation to emotional experience and passion. I am borrowing from Reed's and Baudry's observations when they noted that André Green followed the classical French categories that divided affects into three categories: feelings, emotions, and passion. *Feelings* relate to what Green calls the psychic representation of the drives, meaning the drive as it is felt in the mind; *emotions* (or emotional experience as I refer to it throughout this text) refers to "the sense of internal movement in search of the satisfying object". Passion, which Reed and Baudry note is encountered more often in borderline patients, is an attempt at filling in the absence left behind by the unrepresented object. It is therefore the impossible demand that a materially real object, i.e., one's spouse, substitute for that unrepresented object. I will explain *passion* further. See Reed & Baudry, 2005, pp. 136–137. See also Green, 1986, 1999b, 2005.

2 From Lewis Carroll's *Alice's Adventures in Wonderland*.
3 It goes without saying here, as Ogden (2003) reminds us, that for Bion, thinking involves thoughts and emotions, and, properly speaking, to think one's thoughts entails being able to represent emotions as opposed to evacuating them into symptoms, including behavior and character defenses, or as in the case of Ms. C and her analyst, T(−H).
4 Which for Bion may very well be a battle situation. Many of the senior officers he witnessed sending soldiers to their deaths were certainly portrayed by Bion as stupid and arrogant in his accounts of the war. And I am certain he would not have shied away from describing himself in these terms due to his own guilt about his role in his friends' deaths, as I described in Chapter 1.
5 I will describe the unfolding of the remaining sessions of my vignette with Ms. C in the same detailed back and forth manner to try and show the reader the words she and I both used and how they were experienced and transformed, as closely as possible to what transpired.
6 The analyst has many such thoughts throughout the week, not all of them intrusive, and varying in degree of resonance in terms of helping him organize the way he may experience a particular clinical moment with the patient. All of these thoughts make up his reverie if he is able to conceive of them as such; otherwise, they remain undreamt and only intrude, i.e., become persecutory. When thought of as reverie by the analyst, such thoughts then act as selected facts that shed important light on what is transpiring unconsciously in interaction with the patient, as was the case with the flat-tire memory. I discuss reverie in more detail in Chapters 3 and 4.

Chapter 6

Is it beautiful inside? Transformations in negative hallucinosis and the claustrum

Mr. W

Mr. W felt nervous in the session with me. The previous night he had had a dream that left him feeling anxious. He was back at his old job, and his bosses hated him because he was lazy. Because of this hatred, his colleagues didn't want to be around him. He had no more to say about the dream directly, but he followed it up by adding that at the moment he was feeling anxious. He thought it was the hangover from the weed he had smoked the night before. He then said that his days were empty, and that he had no purpose or aim in his life. Smoking weed gave him "something to look forward to", a sense of a before and after, a present and a future to his day. I responded that he felt he was anxious from the weed hangover, but he was also describing a dream that left him feeling anxious, about his bosses not liking him or hating him, leading to his being rejected all around. It seemed to me that he had no place to go in his dream, like in his waking life, and weed gave him a place to go and be. He responded by saying he also felt anxious with me because he believed I expected him to do all the talking, and if he did not keep the conversation going, I wouldn't have anything to say about him. I responded by saying that he felt that I was like a boss that demanded that he do a lot of work, if not I would be angry at him and hate him, leaving him without any support. He responded by saying that this was "the implication" of his dream, but then added that *he felt confused* and noticed that I often made his dreams about myself. I silently noted that he may have felt I was drawing his attention to me as a concrete object as opposed to *his feelings* about me. In other words, my transference interpretation affirmed his belief that he had to keep the conversation going in a way that would be interesting *to me* if he wanted me to be interested in him. Noticing his anxiety and wanting to turn down the temperature in the room to help contain the emotions, I said I could see how he felt I was making his dream about myself, but that maybe the dream had in common the anxiety he could feel in other places with people, including me. He was telling me that here, like in the dream, he felt it was his job to keep his boss happy and keep the conversation/ workflow going and not be "lazy". I added that I thought that psychotherapy was about allowing the two people involved to be okay if they had nothing to say or think about at the moment, and to say something when they felt they had something they

DOI: 10.4324/9781003520740-7

wanted to say, without feeling the pressure of job performance. He seemed relieved at this, *but then annoyed*, and proceeded to correct me by saying that he was not worried about *job performance* in the dream, just about being hated. I asked why he was hated, and he said he didn't know, but when there were silences (now he himself brought the dream and our experience in the room together) he felt a void (his word), which was quickly filled in by hatred. He thought that I must hate him and didn't want to talk with him, and this reminded him of his parents. They were both educators, interested in understanding themselves, but never their own unwanted son. When he was very young his parents divorced, just to then abdicate responsibility for him because of what he was a reminder of. I said he must have felt he had to do all the work with his parents to keep them interested enough in him as their son to want to stay together as his parents. But they hadn't stayed together, and he was telling me in so many words that he felt they hated him because he reminded them of their marriage. He said that sounded correct, and the session ended a few minutes later. What went uninterpreted, because I lacked an understanding of it at the moment though intuited, was that the hatred that filled in the void—the Greenian passion (1986, 1999a, 2005)—was not his parents but his own, projected into his parents, at feeling dropped by them so early on in his life, dropped by a father he described as excessively self-involved and a mother preoccupied with lovers that Mr. W would often find wandering in his house throughout his childhood. These moments of hatred, flashes really, that were not given the time and space in the psyche to develop before they were projected into the parents, his boss, or me, made up the turbulence underneath that moment of confusion before telling me that like his parents I was making his dream(s) about myself, and his annoyance prior to correcting me about the dream. It is here that the rage, the infant and the child's *passion*, meets the dead mother in the absence of an object representation to hold it and keep the child's burgeoning subjectivity from entering the void that the mother has become.

Mr. W said before the session's end that as a child and indeed all of his life he had to imagine that "everything was all right", and that his parents did love and care about him, contrary to what he felt to be true. But he could not shake the more powerful sense on the periphery that they hated him, something he only came to be convinced of as he grew older. I replied that, as a kid and young man, he needed to create an alternative reality that would help him keep his emotions together and that this continued as an adult. In this way, he protected himself and his parents from his hatred, but the hatred and anxious feelings still seeped through, no matter how much he tried to cut them out of him. And indeed, Mr. W came to see me, now in his 60s, believing he had been severed from his own genitals, an area of his body he felt was anesthetized, and was being persecuted by a conspiracy of artists and performers who sent him coded messages of hatred through the television, humiliating and torturing him.

T(−H) and the claustrum

Donald Meltzer's concept of "the claustrum" (1992) refers to a "place" that is created in the infant and young child's phantasy, latent in the infantile part of the adult psyche, and experienced throughout life as a claustrophobic state of mind where proto-emotions including inchoate anxieties are trapped and experienced untransformed. The subject comes to live in this place, a place that is not only a way of designating an internal "space" but also an outward experience of the world that passes for authentic but that is nevertheless constructed by the projection of unassimilable beta-elements offering nothing less than the gratification of a hallucinated bottle of milk (in reference to Ms. C from the previous chapter). This mental state that can come to overlap with external reality has as its developmental sources early tendencies that were (negatively) nurtured in the young psyche as it learned to grapple with the inner world of sensations, emotions, and anxieties it encountered, usually in relation to its primary objects. By this I mean that instead of learning from experience, the claustrum is a result of *unlearning* from experience, of the negativizing effect of evacuating emotions rather than transforming them into usable, thinkable, and dreamable feelings.[1]

Meltzer describes in detail how these unformulated proto-emotions and anxieties are related to the infant and young child's own body, which over the course of early development becomes intimately linked with phantasies of the maternal body. Meltzer locates these experiences along the trajectory of Freud's psychosexual zones, oral, anal, and phallic/genital. Thus, the infant develops phantasies to organize their experience with the maternal breast, genitals, and anus. At this level of experience, each one of these zones is felt to be a place inside of which the infant lives because the infant projectively (intrusively) identifies his proto-emotional parts into them. Put another way, the infant injects their experience, and with it themselves, into their proto-imaginings of these parts of the mother, who they can only imagine in terms of their own inner state. The infant and young child do this out of the anxieties aroused from coming into contact with these parts of the mother's body, an awareness of which is part phylogenetically pre-determined and part acquired from experience with the actual mother and her body. So the pleasurable sensation of the breast creates a heavenly existence and a heavenly state of mind; the unbearable greediness of the genitals are a form of purgatory for the infant; the maternal anus evokes a form of hell, where the dirtiness associated becomes symbolically equated with the infant's and child's own bad or dirty feelings and the anxieties are of being sucked in or expelled, deprived, or destroyed. In this way, all the proto-emotions become symbolically equated to what these zones of the maternal body represent (rudimentarily) for the infant, and so all experience and phantasy in the claustrum, which is what these zones become, are T(−H). It is, writes Meg Harris Williams, "the world of the negative—in the Bionic sense of the antithesis to thinking and emotional experience, and the perverse areas are 'anti-emotions' rather than hostile or destructive emotions requiring to be integrated" (2022, p. 59).

In a general sense, the anxieties stimulated and managed through the projection into these internal zones of the mother have to do with the infant's attempts at managing and organizing his own archaic and chaotic bodily sensations in relation to the mother, who from the infant's perspective is awe-inspiring and beautiful.

But the mother's beauty, from the vertex of the infant's all-encompassing uncon-scious, that is, from O, renders her a sublime object, beyond the reach of represen-tation and in that way, terrifying. This Meltzer (Meltzer & Williams, 1988/2018) calls the *aesthetic conflict*. "This beautiful object", the infant asks, "is it beautiful *inside*?" In this way, the early subject comes face to face with the black box that is the mother's internal world. Like the psychoanalyst, she comes and goes as she pleases, leaving the infant and the patient perplexed and anxious about the reasons. In *The Apprehension of Beauty*, Meltzer writes,

> The ordinary beautiful devoted mother presents to her ordinary beautiful baby a complex object of overwhelming interest, both sensual and infrasensual. Her outward beauty, concentrated as it must be in her breast and face, complicated in each case by her nipples and her eyes, bombards him with an emotional experi-ence of a passionate quality, the result of his being able to see these objects as "beautiful". But the meaning of his mother's behaviour, of the appearance and disappearance of the breast and of the light in her eyes, of a face over which emotions pass like the shadows of clouds over the landscape, are unknown to him.
>
> (Meltzer & Williams, 1988/2018, p. 22)

The terrifying, yet irresistible question "is it beautiful inside?" ushers in the possibility of the depressive position where the tension between the inside and the outside of experience can be tolerated. Meg Harris Williams reminds us that for Meltzer, the absent object cannot be conceived of without at first an apprehension of this present object, an object that arouses a tremendous ambivalence. She writes, "it is the present object with the unknowable inside that stimulates turbulence and the temptation to retreat into the paranoid-schizoid mode" (2022, p. 47), the mode of projection, splitting, disobjectalization, attacks on linking, and negative hallu-cination. This unknowability takes us back to the terrain of curiosity and knowing described by Bion in *On Arrogance* (1958a) and in the previous chapter, where the tensions generated between the ineffable inside and outside of the object stimulate curiosity and attempts at knowing that can range from depressive position and healthy, imaginative identifications (reverie), to intrusive and controlling identifica-tions stimulated by the intolerable black-box unknowing of the paranoid-schizoid positions (Williams, 2022, p. 47). I will say more about intrusive identifications (as opposed to healthy, communicative projective identifications) later.

The phantasy partition into psychosexual and geographic locations for the sub-ject's proto-emotions and anxieties to me is less important than the fact of the crea-tion of a claustrum atmosphere inside the mind that spills into the experience of the world in which the subject moves. In fact, the quality and characteristics of these zones—in Bion's military cartography from the First World War he might have said "the ground features"—at first glance seems more relevant to understanding patients who are functioning at a more psychotic level. These features track more easily with delusional anxieties of bodily fragmentation, for example, around the genitals and the anus, and in patients who live in a world of sado-masochistic per-secution and narcissism (greedy genital impulses). However, when the analyst's ear is appropriately tuned some of these same features may also be detected in characterologically non-psychotic patients who nevertheless grapple with primi-tive anxieties of a similar nature, despite the layers of secondary process that may obscure them from simple sight. As I will try and show next, the detailed terms of Meltzer's psychic cartography with its related psychosexual ground features nev-ertheless offer the analyst valuable clinical insight on patients across the spectrum of pathology in as much as they help give name and representation to the degree and nature of the anxieties and the "unfathomable" phantasies attached to them.

As for Mr. W, who felt severed from his penis and sadistically persecuted by the people on the television, Meltzer's detailed descriptions are useful. Mr. W's anxie-ties about sexuality, exacerbated in his childhood by both the lack of a father with whom to speak and learn from about his sensations and impulses, and a sexually overly intrusive, yet coy mother who kept a cold distance, contributed to a zonal confusion about his own bodily experiences and a stunted, if not disabled, ability to represent his proto-emotions. In the clinical excerpt I presented earlier, after I connected his conscious experience of me as demanding he do all the work in the session to his dream of his boss and colleagues hating him because he was "lazy", Mr. W understood "the implication" but immediately collapsed me into the figure of the boss in the dream, rather than preserving the boss and me as representations of each other (or both of us as representations of his own self-hatred and rage). He subsequently felt that I was making his dream about me, just as his boss made work about his, the boss', needs of him. The boss and I were concretely folded into each other in One Reality, as persecutors who called him "lazy". In this way, the internal world of the claustrum folded out into the here and now environment of the consulting room. Through T(−H), "the implication" of my interpretation becomes negatively hallucinated, that is, the link made between me standing in for his boss in the dream, that Mr. W can see and acknowledge, becomes instantly erased, and now I *am* the boss in One Reality, who he cannot see but experiences. Through T(−H) the image of the boss disappears, but I take on his attributes. The caesura between the inner and outer world is eclipsed, the internal world pouring forth and becoming the outer world, encircling the patient who is now persecuted, as well as the analyst who is now the object of suspicion by the patient and whose very actions confirm that suspicion. We are in the claustrum.

We can also see here the presence of the "greedy genital impulses" that Meltzer placed in "purgatory". In Mr. W's lived experience, they exist but are split off in the concrete form of his severed penis and his perennial awaiting the return of sexual feelings to his genitals. In the session as well as in the dream, they are intrusively identified into me and the boss, so that we hold all the genital greed, demanding he put out, and he is persecuted by it and us. The "hell" of the maternal rectum was an area of fascination for Mr. W, who as an adolescent fantasied about sadistically penetrating and debasing women through the anus. It reminded him of his mother's humiliating submission to her lovers, which was the only way he could make sense out of aesthetic conflict comprised by the fact that she was both sexually seductive *and* conveyed the idea that she did not take pleasure in sex. Like the "conservative" (Meltzer, 1992, p. 119) anus that retains, Mr. W's mother deprived him of warmth, sensuality, and knowledge of sex, just as he deprived his boss and me of his work. The claustrum in the session and of his psyche was like a work environment where he was constantly under threat of being fired (expelled, evacuated) for being depriving and controlling, and where he in turn was sadistically dominated and deprived. Mr. W had at one point in his life been a stage performer, but over the past few years the aesthetic and creative impulse had "disappeared" in the same way his genital feelings had, and the stage from which he was able to retain some connection to his inner world had transformed into a nightmare of persecution from the world of performers that would have been his peers. The realm of beauty had become the world of shit. But most importantly, the claustrum itself as both a *means* of evacuation and *a refuge* was closely related to the "heavenly" compartment of the mother's breast, facilitating a state of grace for the subject who escapes into the sensual engulfment of primary narcissism, where the external object no longer needs to be reckoned with and represented, and can instead be projected into and controlled narcissistically and intrusively. At-one with the object, the patient is in a state of O, immersed in a reflective experience of their own proto-emotions with no boundaries, beginning or end, and yielding pleasure (even if painful) in the place of understanding (Bion, 1970).

The extent to which an understanding of the claustrophobic anxieties contained in the chambers of the claustrum can be communicated helpfully to the patient and in what form is something every analyst has to consider when working with psychotic patients. A significant feature of the claustrum is the environment produced by the hyperbolic loop of $T(-H)$, where the act of interpreting, as was saw previously, recreates the intrusive object the patient fends off through $T(-H)$. It is useful, however, to be able to listen for these anxieties recurring in the material at different moments and to think of them as a guide to know where one is located in the patient's transference, including the nature of the anxieties stimulated in the here and now of the interaction. The analyst can in this way get a sense as to what the patient is struggling to put into words and respond accordingly, always with the objective in mind of providing a container for these anxieties so that they can be transformed away from creating a claustrum in the patient's mind and out of the analyst and the analysis, and in the direction of a container which would transform these intrusive identifications in the analyst's mind into communicative, realistic projective identifications, as I will explain later. Interpreting the transference in a more saturated way can lead to $T(-H)$ where the links with reality become more tenuous and collapse, as we saw with Mr. W. But using the material to locate oneself within the transference and interpreting from within it can lead to a more containing atmosphere that can gradually replace the claustrum and allow for the flow of communication of proto-emotions to continue and the subsequent development of the capacity to represent them through experiences in the room coupled with words. Here Ferro, writing about the tyranny of the superego when the superego is an artifact of the analyst's intrusive curiosity into the patient, recreating a $-(♀♂)$, is instructive:

> This of course gives rise to a significant problem of technique: does the analyst interpret these two modalities (saturated versus "open" interpretations) exhaustively in transference terms, or alternately, can the analyst "tolerate" learning from the patient the interpretative style most suited to that particular patient at that particular moment, and then transform his or her interpretive style and attitude in such a way that the analytic superego and the superego of the relational field uniting the analyst and patient are transformed with them?
>
> (Ferro, 2005, p. 71; my parentheses)

In this way, I may decide against interpreting that today Mr. W is afraid my silence means that like his boss I am asking him to work more. Instead, I might think about being more talkative in the session to help repair a container where he can feel less internal pressure to balance the weight of *our* marriage on his shoulders, as he may have felt with his mother and father. At the same time, I may be alerted to listening for ways in which I might be speaking to him that have been placing undue weight on his capacity to understand and have thus stimulated fears that he would be fired or gotten rid of by one of his parents or his boss. Was I speaking too quickly? Was Mr. W picking up an impatience in my voice, for example, and if so, had I unknowingly been feeling inpatient with him? Was my impatience the manifestation of a particular object relationship being enacted without being dreamt, existing at the level of O and unreflected on? Or was my impatience with him an impatience in the field between us, the impatience being my bodily manifestation of the O between Mr. W and I, something unrepresented and trapped, waiting to break out to be born(e) into language? Thus, insight into the unconscious, unrepresented anxieties of entrapment, expulsion, humiliation, and abandonment in the anal chamber of the claustrum can inform me on the need to recalibrate my psychoanalytic demeanor and allow both of us more space to think about his and our emotions in the room together.

On frying giant frozen oranges

To this end, it is important to highlight the *phantasy* aspect of the claustrum. It exists as a "place" in the mind of the individual only in the sense that it is the internal state of mind that results from the individual's failed attempts at processing, metabolizing, and containing intense phantasies involving proto-anxieties and impulses. For any number of combined reasons, these phantasies have not been worked-through in any meaningful way that could drive psychological development forward through the formation and institution of conscious and unconscious thinking (varying in degrees of sophistication from phantasies to ideas) that could serve as containers for developmental experiences. Instead of ideas that could hold and process experiences, leading to the internalization of a good internal object and environment, a claustrophobic object is created, a claustrum. This in turn sets up a claustrophobic internal setting. It is claustrophobic because the parts of the self that are contained in the phantasies are trapped and concretized in the object, rather than worked-through in the way they would with a containing object. Several contributing factors are at play here: the intolerable anxieties, sensations, and impulses (all proto at this level) in need of representation are dealt with by intrusive identification (Meltzer, 1992), rather than by realistic projective identification (Bion, 1962a, 1962b). Another factor, of course, is the analyst's receptivity to the intrusively identified material, which is impaired when the analyst's defenses are activated to try to contain it. It is not as much that the patient "attacks the analyst's links" through the intrusive identification, but rather that the anxiety that is generated in the analyst when coming into contact with the patient's warded off and unrepresented material triggers in the analyst his own processes of de-linking in the service of relieving psychic pressure.

As I mentioned earlier, the distinct nature of intrusive (projective) identification was made by Meltzer, who specified a modality that distinguished itself from the projective identification that Bion termed "real" for of its communicative and developmentally appropriate value. In the last chapter, I described how Bion stressed the communicative function of this type of projective identification in *On Arrogance*, an elaboration he made on Klein's understanding of the defense as a form of controlling the object from within. Meltzer's intrusive identification is more in line with Klein's initial formulation, except that it emphasizes the extreme nature of the projective identificatory activity, in a way that is also in keeping with T(−H) as I am conceiving of it here.[2] In T(−H), the unbearable proto-emotions are expelled from the psyche in such an extreme way that they become transformed into a negative of themselves, an absence that relegates the involved experience to the realm of meaninglessness and concreteness. The world the individual creates to place their experience is a "nowhere world" (Meltzer, 1992, p. 118). When the individual employs intrusive identification as a means of ridding the psyche of the excess of stimulus produced by experience, they create an internal environment of uninterpretable and as such impenetrable objects that they feel trapped by, and we could say, within. I would like to reemphasize here that we are talking about a phantasy and that this newly generated internal environment takes place in the subject's own mind, and it is through this experience that he interacts with the object and the world connected to it. It may and can be induced in the object-analyst in the form of intrusive (projective) identification, but it starts and ends in the mind of the projector with or without the analyst as a medium. As such there is a *phantasy* of ridding the psyche through intrusive identification, but nothing is gotten rid of except for an awareness of the source of anxiety since the situation has now been drained of meaning. But the anxiety persists, lodged in the nowhere objects that make up the nowhere world. If the object is an egg that the proto-psyche creates in order to inject itself into, to be gestated and then hatched in an evolved and transformed state, the pressure of the injection, and the frightening content of the DNA being transferred is of such intensity and density that the egg freezes and never comes to term. The communication-transformation devolves into an evacuation. Lacking, then, in symbolic transformation, the proto-emotions cannot be "dreamed" and cannot therefore move from basic primary process level "thinking" into representational elaboration proper of the secondary processes. The individual then experiences themselves as locked into this world, awaiting perhaps the warmth of maternal reverie that the psychoanalyst can provide to bring the frozen egg to term. In dreamlife, the claustrum may appear in a non-dream, a nightmare, or a hallucination in dreaming (Bion, 1958–1979). Mr. W's dream of his boss and colleagues is an example of a hallucination in dreaming where the claustrum takes the place of the setting. Next is another example of a claustrum dream, this one from an extremely anxious, neurotic patient:

> Ms. A, an anxious young woman dreamt of being inside a freezing cold, oval-shaped room. She was in the center, and was surrounded by giant, frozen, oval-shaped oranges. She felt extremely anxious.

Ms. A had no associations and saw no connection between this dream and the news she had just received from her gynecologist of pre-cancerous cells in her uterus, which she told me about later in the session. She had been shaken by the dream, which she remembered vividly, but could not think of the images as anything other than what they obviously appeared as: giant frozen oranges. She could only express the pervasive feeling of anxiety that continued into her waking state.

In terms of the claustrum, we might think that through intrusive (as opposed to communicative or realistic) projective identification, Ms. A created an object into which she projected her unwanted parts, if initially as a way of communicating them to herself, ultimately as a way of controlling them by placing them elsewhere or in the other. She ended up trapped in this object (she was in the center of an oval-shaped room, the place where these unwanted experiences landed) because she was unable to truly get rid of these parts (as they were a part of her). These unwanted and untransformed parts persecuted her, as they un-wanted her (the quality of unwantedness did not get erased) and were so bad that she feared they damaged the object who would now retaliate. In response, she evacuated again, until the concrete (Bion's bizarre) objects surrounded and entrapped her. Ms. A was now in the looking-glass world of the claustrum and of T(−H). The experiences evacuated were so crude, so untransformed and unrepresented, that they existed in unmodified and concrete ways in the object, constraining its ability to transform into a container in her mind.

In this way, the giant, frozen oranges became the negative of her (feared) cancerous eggs, which she could not allow herself to think about but anxiously stared back at her. The ghost of her anxious inhibitions around sexuality were enclosed in the images of the frozen oranges/eggs, inside the cancerous ovary/room. Ms. A inhibited her sexuality to avoid contracting HPV, which she feared would lead to cancer and result in the punishment she felt she deserved for being able to win her mother's favoritism if she were to conceive babies when her older sister, who indeed did have her uterus removed because of cancer, could not. We can see now that the claustrum state of mind, set out in the dream, involves what Meltzer (1992) designated as the genital chamber. Here, Ms. A's "greedy" sexual impulses needed to be frozen in limbo lest she destroy the maternal object, split between the defeated older sister and the idealized mother for whose exclusive love she yearned.

A conceptual question arises—because we are speaking of images of frozen oranges, would this not be a regular dream composed of symbolism, or at worst, transformations in *positive* hallucinosis? I think, in most cases the presence of dream images is not enough for deciding if a dream is a real dream or a non-dream, or whether we are speaking of T(+H) or T(−H), without considering the subject's relation to the images in the dream, which is often a reflection of the function the images perform. Often, I think, our dreams contain hallucinations that we brush away or *cannot* think about, rather than not remember due to repression of their troublesome symbolic content. In the case of Ms. A, a patient whose neurotic (or non-psychotic) functioning activated her psychotic functioning, her anxiety around sexuality was highly pitched due to its linkage to annihilation, her sister's and her own. Rather than symbols that gazed back at her enigmatically (Laplanche, 1999), suggesting interpretation and stimulating curiosity, association, or even forgetting as they might in any neurotic subject, they remained in her waking life as signs that pointed to nothingness, to blankness in her mind creating immense anxiety. It was up to me, in my mind as I wrote my notes after the session, to make and dream the connections to her story that, outside of the immediate field of anxiety, came to me without memory or desire.

Meltzer clarifies that the claustrum refers to a *part* of the individual and an *area* of her experience and not the total individual in their total experience, a clarification I also made in the previous chapter regarding T(−H). Another way of speaking about this is to refer to "the part of the personality living in the claustrum" (Meltzer, 1992, p. 120). However, the claustrum state of mind, in some people, can be projected into a general entrapping and pessimistic outlook in life that indeed seems all-encompassing, which in the psychotic subject takes the form of a delusional system. In this way, the "nowhere world" is not only the claustrum but the place the subject escapes to from the entrapping claustrum itself (ibid, p. 119), "out of the frying pan, into the frying pan", so to speak.

Heaven can't wait

Such was the case with Ms. Q, who retreated into a nowhere world of self-stimulation and nothingness, leading to disturbing feelings of disintegration, in an attempt to escape a nowhere world of intrusive or unresponsive objects that stimulated an intense anxiety of annihilation.

At a large family dinner, Ms. Q and her husband were seated with the children at one end of the table, while her adult siblings, their partners, and her parents were seated at the other end. She quietly observed them conversing among themselves and noted that they were seated where the food was, far away from where she and her husband were seated. She didn't feel anything, or at least in telling me about this, didn't *remember* feeling anything. At the dinner, she noticed her father seemingly annoyed when she had to reach over him to get food. She also noticed the expression on her own husband's face, which she interpreted as his feelings of exclusion and disconcertion over having been "exiled" to the kids' table. She did not remember, however, having any feelings of her own about this. Here we might say, given what she thought she saw in her husband's and father's expressions, that she had felt the stirring of *emotion*, in André Green's sense of the word, but not *feelings*, as she did not attach meaning to her experience. My sense is that she immediately began *detaching* meaning from her experience, i.e., began a T(−H), as soon as representations threatened to make it known to her. This vague stirring of emotion portended for her a sense of disorganization which she attempted to keep at bay by making herself feel mostly nothing, *all the while she observed the formation of feelings of concern and irritation on her husband's and her father's faces*, a sign for me that she was already engaged in projecting and expelling bits and pieces of her experience. She next found herself fidgeting and then fussing over the kids she felt it was now her job to take care of (she now observed needs *in the children*) rather than having her own needs for adult conversation met. She sensed that in fidgeting and managing the kids she was getting away from an internal agitation of some sort, something we had talked about before that she did and that might function as a way of placing (projecting) outside of herself the threat of disorganization, "doing something" to keep herself mended by externalizing the internal fidgeting. Her noticing this vague sense of something purposeful to her fidgeting, I think, was a sign that her alpha-functioning was being stimulated to help her contain the emotions by transforming them into feelings she could readily understand and manage. Nonetheless, the internal fidgeting (the turbulence) increasingly stirred within her as she saw her family conversing and laughing, and her father and husband growing more and more irritated and disconcerted. She found herself ordering one martini, then another, and then another. Now she found herself in the bathroom, vomiting, until she was taken home by her husband.

Ms. Q prefaced this account by saying she was embarrassed to talk to me about it, and after ending it said she felt a great deal of shame. One of her siblings was short with her on the phone the day after, and her spouse complained that she had left the lights on at home. This made her want to break down and cry, and pour herself into him, but upon seeing him critical of her she instead shut down and "went inside of herself", as we often spoke about in sessions. She was left uneasy when afterwards her husband returned from another room with a darkened look on his face. She then said to me, "yes, I decide to recluse myself, I don't want to see anyone, I don't want to talk to him anymore, I just want to be alone". I responded that when she feels she has emotions that she does not understand, but feels she needs to communicate, and feels the other person will be critical or blame her, the emotions become worse, more disorganizing, and she looks for a way to change them or to get rid of them, either through fidgeting or by drinking. But when that doesn't do it, the disorganized feelings can become too much for her to handle, and she might lose control of them, unless she withdraws and becomes a recluse. I added that perhaps to be a recluse, to go deep inside of herself in those moments was a way of stopping the "reck-loose" emotions inside of her from taking over. But then she loses touch with everything inside and outside of her and is paralyzed by fear.

Ms. Q had come to see me for analysis some six months earlier, and we began at a frequency of three times a week. Despite the intensity of her emotions, this frequency seemed like the appropriate dosage given her combined need for distance and contact. Early on we decided against her using the couch because of the dissociated state the reclined position instantly induced in her when she first laid down. That day, she was barely able to leave my office, feeling as if she had physically crumbled and then imploded, reduced to a state of absolute helplessness. This state, however, was subsequently induced at other moments when Ms. Q felt I was unresponsive to her, for example, if I repeatedly did not respond as she hoped when trying to enlist me to openly take her side in a situation where she felt she was being neglected or intruded on by her family. She was often very watchful of me, in a way that made me feel observed and that I imagined had the function of inhibiting my ability to observe her. I often felt overly cautious in what I said to her, careful to not make a misplaced remark or to not intrude with my interpretations, which she experienced early in our work as gaslighting. She explained that my emphasis on her internal experience had the effect of making her feel that I was denying the reality of her external perceptions, an effect that while not uncommon in many people, I think was accentuated by her symbolic equation of me as the dangerous incarnation of her own terrifying and unrepresented internal experience. Transference interpretations in this light were construed as delegitimizing and blaming her for her pain. In moments such as these when Ms. Q could not make sense out of my actions, she would become very disconcerted and suspicious and experience herself detaching in session, barely able to muster the words, "It doesn't matter anyway. Nothing matters anyway. What's the point anyway". Her body might become completely limp, and although she would not be able to say what she felt, her facial expression would convey utter desolation. She would remain motionless, speechless, and unreachable for the remainder of the hour. I felt in these moments as if I was witnessing in real time an incredibly painful emotional collapse, triggered by the experience of being in relation to an object whose meaning she could not understand or had any power over. When she was able to stay regulated in such moments, she could use intrusive identification to do so, inducing in me a feeling of being controlled through the way I was watched or through the dramatic negative impact of what I said or didn't say. Often, the manner in which she spoke to me felt calculated to elicit a specific response, one that would give her evidence for something she was consciously or unconsciously suspecting. Ms. Q was open about this, and we talked about her way of speaking to me when at the start of her analysis she described the conversation style of her family of origin as strategic and "Game-of-Thrones-like". I understood and learned to accept this early in our work, an understanding that helped soften my countertransference anxiety around it, allowing me to keep in mind that Ms. Q felt terribly threatened and constrained by me, which in turn helped me contain her need to keep me under watch.

I was perceived as a threat by Ms. Q when she saw me as unsettlingly mysterious, as when I needed to cancel a session. At times I felt it necessary to explain my reasons for canceling, only to find my explanations subject to more scrutiny, as she suspected I was trying to pull the wool over her eyes to disguise my secret feelings of being burdened by her. Here is Meltzer's aesthetic conflict again. Ms. Q asks the idealized maternal object, "why are you leaving me?" hoping to receive an assurance that she will not be abandoned and that the object that is beautiful on the outside is indeed beautiful on the inside. But the anxiety of abandonment that this aesthetic object induces in Ms. Q stimulates an overpowering need to protect herself, and she begins to withdraw from the object by subjecting her links to it to T(−H), "What is the point of analysis anyway? Why do I even come here anyway?" This had the effect of negativizing her emotions connected to the object and of furthering her retreat inside of herself into a place where she could hide, a retreat into Meltzer's heavenly maternal breast chamber of the claustrum. Here she hoped to feel safe and not need the external object as she was at-one with the sensual surround of nothingness that she had enclosed herself in. However, this claustrum by its nature is not a place that can contain her experience, as it is constructed out of intrusive identifications meant to manage affects too intense, too terrifying to be transformed into feelings that could be understood and felt. The claustrum becomes a form of beta-screen, the thoughts that could not be tolerated converted backward into an envelope of sensuous elements, through another round of T(−H). But because the beta-envelope cannot contain—that is transform—the turbulent emotional storm, the latter is subjected to another dose of T(−H) leading Ms. Q to become more disorganized as a way of further dispersing the contents of this intense inner experience. Instead of an unconscious that expands, transforming psychic pain into thinkable and tolerable thoughts (alpha-elements) that enrich personal experience and bring Ms. Q closer to lived, emotional truth, it is the claustrum that expands, with unconscious dreaming being replaced by T(−H).

Under pressure

I'd like to change gears slightly before concluding this chapter by turning to a film that I feel movingly and compellingly captures the retreat into T(−H) and the claustrum, the 2022 film *Aftersun* written and directed by Charlotte Wells. In this film, an 11-year-old Scottish girl named Sophie (Frankie Corio) is on a vacation with her young father, Calum (Paul Mescal), in a resort town in southern Türkiye. Calum lives in London, away from his daughter who lives with her mother in Scotland, though the divorced parents are still close and say they love each other in the presence of Sophie. On the cusp of puberty, Sophie is curious about the world of older boys and girls and is excited to be around her father on what looks like their yearly holiday alone together. Throughout the film, we see young Sophie and father eating, swimming, walking, playing cards together, having close conversation, and rubbing sunscreen on each other's backs and legs, in the kind of father-daughter intimacy that betrays both Sophie's devotion toward her father as well as her embarrassment and restlessness for hanging out with the older kids. Calum is appropriately mindful of boundaries, aware of his daughter's growing curiosity in what the older boys and girls at the resort are up to, and gradually allows them to hang out. However, we see that Sophie, intensely alert and curious as any young girl at that age, senses something wrong in her father, causing shadows to pass over his face "like clouds over the landscape" (Meltzer & Williams, 1988/2018, p. 22). We can sense her wondering what it means that he becomes spontaneously, deeply immersed in the patterns of Tai-Chi forms on the balcony of their hotel room or in the middle of the street or on the side of the road. She is confused and hurt when he, taken by surprise, rejects her invitation to sing "Losing My Religion" at karaoke with him one night under the exposing gaze of the guests at the hotel. Later, on the day of his 31st birthday, while on a day trip to an ancient ruin, Sophie surprises him again by enlisting a group of tourists to sing, "For he's a jolly good fellow" while he, away from the crowd and up on a top step turns, the expression on his face darkened, covered in the shadow of the trees.

Throughout the vacation, Sophie carries her father's camcorder and playfully records spontaneous moments between the two, along with herself making funny faces and dancing in front of the lens. In one of these recorded scenes, she playfully asks her father where, at age 11—her age—he thought he would be at 31, the age he was turning that day. We see from Calum's avoidant and silently irritated response subtle signs of a man quietly and deeply depressed, withdrawn into a world that he struggled to keep from his young daughter in order not to impinge on her budding excitement for life and growth, and on one of the few times in the year that they spent alone together. But Sophie *sees all this, even though she doesn't see it*. We know she sees the self-help books and that her father still smokes cigarettes despite his warnings to her that they are deadly. Her questions to Calum betray innocence, curiosity, confusion, and a subdued but anxious need to understand—Bion's stupidity, curiosity, and arrogance—questions such as why he still tells her mother he loves her, and where he imagined himself to be at 31 from the perspective of his 11-year-old self. Gestating in these queries is the deeper concern of, "is it beautiful inside?", a question with which Sophie ever gently but desperately reaches out to touch her father's hidden self. She "knows" Calum lied about having a scuba license in order to go out on a dive, and she "unknows" and keeps unformulated on another level what she fears will break through into conscious representation, that he is happiest when immersed underwater, deep in the dark seas of his mind, plunged into the sensations of flowing forms, sounds, and substances.

Sophie watches as Calum struggles and ultimately declines to buy an expensive and beautiful Turkish carpet he is strongly drawn to but cannot reasonably afford, and as viewers we watch him secretly return and put it on his credit card, presumably sinking himself deeper into debt. Interspersed throughout the film, we see adult Sophie (Celia Rowlson-Hall) looking back on this last trip with her father. Now Calum's age, she is sitting on her bed, bare feet resting on that Turkish carpet as she thinks back. At other moments, she is reaching into the videos still trying to find her father in his darkness, a darkness that now appears to have become her own. It is her 31st birthday, she awakens troubled, we hear a baby in the background and her partner in bed, lovingly and reassuringly saying, "happy birthday, Sophie", as Sophie marches away from view. In another scene, on the night after rejecting Sophie's invitation to karaoke, we see Calum on the beach, briskly marching into the black waters in the middle of the night, with the determination of a man looking to sink forever into the dark, bottomless void.

But in the most important scenes scattered throughout the film, we catch glimpses of Calum's silhouette, vanishing and reappearing within the dark, sensational sur-round of physical, boundless stimulation, inundated and muted by agonizing joy as he mindlessly lets himself go to the all-encompassing music of a dark and strobe-lit rave. We catch glimpses of him in faint outlines, and then he is gone again, only for an impression to reappear in its place, and then another fragment of an image disfigured by the flashing lights and the other forms. We imagine the rave setting is from Sophie's world in the present, places where she now loses herself in search for her father, tracing his form from the crowd of silhouettes always blocking him from view, perhaps a place where 31-year-old Sophie and her 31-year-old father can have a last dance together. Maybe now as an adult, she feels she can be at-one with her father's pain for only a moment before they both disappear back into their own voids. We see Calum on the edge of his bed in the middle of the night, naked, back turned to us, weeping, with loving postcards he had written to Sophie on the floor of the hotel room. We see adult Sophie entering the claustrum rave again and again, each time getting closer and closer, always failing to reach him. Fragments of the music break through like acoustic images, barely audible but transforming into barely discernible, and finally articulate sounds that reach a pitch enabling us to hear pieces of the song in which Calum is encapsulated and at-one. Now Calum is on the hotel dance floor on the last night of their trip, persuading a reluctant 11-year-old Sophie to join him in a last dance, which they share as he clings to her desperately, enraptured by the music, grasping her tightly as her adult self is finally able to grab hold of him in the dark rave, finding and catching him while the words "Turned away, from it all, like a blind man" break through, bit by bit to the surface. Now, both child and adult Sophie are at the rave, in the claustrum with Calum, as she loses hold of him and watches helplessly as he falls back into the void.

In conclusion

Meltzer uses the spacial metaphor of the claustrum to gather into the form of a defense organization some of the psychic processes I have been describing in the preceding chapters and this one related to transformations in hallucinosis and more specifically, transformations in *negative* hallucinosis. The delicate dance of at-onement and devastating loss, between Sophie and Calum in *Aftersun*, between Bion and his comrades chronicled in Chapter 1, and in the many experiences of and with the patients described in these pages, give evidence to how each of them, including the psychoanalyst, has had to grapple with and get to know their own ghost, that part of us that would otherwise, to our impoverishment, fall back into the void.

Notes

1 When, conversely, emotions can be transformed into feelings, they can be thought about and dreamt, and therefore stand as representations of an inner state the subject can use to know something about themselves, rather than experienced concretely, raw, as unfathomable O.
2 In fact, both Klein (1946) and Bion (1962a, 1962b) had already described a form of projective identification that was "excessive".

Epilogue

In August of 2023, I paid a visit to the battleground off of the Amiens-Roye Road, in the Somme near the town of Domart-sur-la-Luce, abutting the River Luce where Bion, on the morning of August 8th, stared paralyzed into his field compass. His tanks lining up beside him, the brothers Sweeting, Hauser, Johnson, Sgt. O'Toole, Cpl. Stone, and Asser waited somewhere nearby. In the 105 years that have passed since that day, the river seems to have grown narrower where it meets the road, transformed into something short of a stream. The plains, knolls, and plateaus on either side are covered in dense, deep grass, with stretches of thick forest rising here and there. Etchings in the ground intimating large ditches, likely created by what now seem ancient bomb blasts, can be discerned underneath plots of soil reused for farming. On this day in August of 2023, the harvest seemed to have just been reaped.

We were headed north toward the town of Amiens to tour the canals and the cathedral in the town center, but before that headed south toward Dodo Wood. Now called Rifle Wood, this is the small forest—larger now since 1918—where some of the fighting during the battle of Amiens occurred and where Bion stopped to regroup with what remained of his men to await orders after the initial assault on August 8th. Halfway between the Luce and Dodo Wood is the Hourges Orchard Cemetery, containing the remains of soldiers from the Canadian 43rd, 58th, and 116th; the Australian 49th and 51st; and the British 1st and 161st battalions, all killed on August 8, 1918. In all, 144 of the 44,000 estimated to have lost their lives that day are interred here. In *War Memoirs*, Bion shows us a picture of the Canadian infantry walking through the skeletal remains of this wood, after the first line of infantry had already passed. German soldiers had been imbedded there before the Allied bombardment prior to their advance, and Bion commented how usually, shelling does little to show its effects on a forest full of trees, but in this picture one could get "a good idea of the intensity of the British bombardment".

Leaving the cemetery that grey and rainy morning, as we were headed toward the car, I remarked that I was a little disappointed that I did not see any poppies in the fields around us, as I had hoped. "Daddy!" I heard, barely finishing my sentence, and looking down saw my daughter's and son's outstretched hands, each with a poppy in the center. "Didn't you see them?" they cried. "They were all over the place!"

DOI: 10.4324/9781003520740-8

References

Abel-Hirsch, N. (2019) *Bion: 365 Quotes*. London: Routledge.

Aisenstein, M. (2020) Repetition and the Compulsion to Repeat, a French Perspective. *International Journal of Psychoanalysis* 101:1203–1214.

Angeloch, D. (2021) The Experience of the First World War in Wilfred Bion's Autobiographical Writings. *The Psychoanalytic Quarterly* 90(1):7–48.

Barahona, R. (2020) Living the Non-Dream: An Examination of the Links Between Dreaming, Enactment, and Transformations in Hallucinosis. *Psychoanalytic Quarterly* 89:689–714.

Barahona, R. (2022) The Hallucinated Field. In *The Post-Bionian Field Theory of Antonino Ferro. Theoretical Analysis and Clinical Application*, edited by H. Levine. London: Routledge, pp. 84–95.

Bell, D. (2022) Psychoanalytic Reflections on the Conditions of Possibility of Human Destructiveness. *International Journal of Psychoanalysis* 103:674–691.

Bergstein, A. (2019) *Bion and Meltzer's Expeditions into Unmapped Mental Life: Beyond the Spectrum in Psychoanalysis*. London: Routledge.

Bergstein, A. (2022) "Truth Shall Spring Out of the Earth . . .": The Analyst as Gatherer of Sense Impressions. *International Journal of Psychoanalysis* 103:246–263.

Bion, W. R. (1957) Differentiation of the Psychotic from the Non-Psychotic Personalities. *International Journal of Psycho Analysis* 38:266–275.

Bion, W. R. (1958a) On Arrogance. In *Complete Works*, VI, edited by C. Mawson. London: Routledge, pp. 131–137. 2014.

Bion, W. R. (1958b) Attacks on Linking. In *Complete Works*, VI, edited by C. Mawson. London: Routledge, pp. 138–152. 2014.

Bion, W. R. (1958–1979) Cogitations. In *Complete Works*, XI, edited by C. Mawson. London: Routledge. 2014.

Bion, W. R. (1962a) A Theory of Thinking. In *Complete Works*, VI, edited by C. Mawson. London: Routledge, pp. 153–161. 2014.

Bion, W. R. (1962b) Learning from Experience. In *Complete Works*, IV, edited by C. Mawson. London: Routledge, pp. 261–365. 2014.

Bion, W. R. (1963) Elements of Psychoanalysis. In *Complete Works*, V, edited by C. Mawson. London: Routledge, pp. 7–86. 2014.

Bion, W. R. (1965) Transformations. In *Complete Works*, V, edited by C. Mawson. London: Routledge, pp. 123–280. 2014.

Bion, W. R. (1967) Second Thoughts. In *Complete Works*, VI, edited by C. Mawson. London: Routledge, pp. 45–202.

Bion, W. R. (1970) Attention and Interpretation. In *Complete Works*, VI, edited by C. Mawson. London: Routledge, pp. 213–330. 2014.

Bion, W. R. (1974) The Brazilian Lectures. In *Complete Works*, VII, edited by C. Mawson. London: Routledge. 2014.

Bion, W. R. (1975) A Memoir of the Future. Book One: The Dream. In *Complete Works*, XII, edited by C. Mawson. London: Routledge. 2014.

Bion, W. R. (1976) Four Discussions. In *Complete Works*, X, edited by C. Mawson. London: Routledge. 2014.

Bion, W. R. (1976–1979) Four Papers. In *Complete Works*, X, edited by C. Mawson. London: Routledge. 2014.

Bion, W. R. (1977a) Taming Wild Thoughts (II) Untitled. In *Complete Works*, X, edited by C. Mawson. London: Routledge. 2014.

Bion, W. R. (1977b) A Memoir of the Future. Book Two: The Past Presented. In *Complete Works*, XIII, edited by C. Mawson. London: Routledge. 2014.

Bion, W. R. (1977–1978) Bion in New York and Sao Paulo. In *Complete Works*, VIII, edited by C. Mawson. London: Routledge. 2014.

Bion, W. R. (1982) The Long Weekend. In *Complete Works*, I, edited by C. Mawson. London: Routledge. 2014.

Bion, W. R. (1985) All My Sins Remembered: Another Part of Life. In *Complete Works*, II, edited by C. Mawson. London: Routledge, pp. 1–77. 2014.

Bion, W. R. (1997) War Memoir. In *Complete Works*, III, edited by C. Mawson. London: Routledge. 2014.

Birksted-Breen, D. (2016) Bi-Ocularity, the Functioning Mind of the Psychoanalyst. *International Journal of Psychoanalysis* 97:25–40.

Bleger, J. (1967) Psycho-Analysis of the Psycho-Analytic Frame. *International Journal of Psychoanalysis* 48:511–519

Botella, C. & Botella, S. (2001) *The Work of Psychic Figurability: Mental States Without Representation*. London: Routledge. 2004.

Brown, L. J. (2005) The Cognitive Effects of Trauma: Reversal of Alpha Function and the Formation of a Beta Screen. *Psychoanalytic Quarterly* 74:397–420.

Brown, L. J. (2012) Bion's Discovery of Alpha Function: Thinking Under Fire on the Battlefield and in the Consulting Room. *International Journal of Psychoanalysis* 93:1191–1214.

Brown, L. J. (2018) Deconstructing Countertransference. *Psychoanalytic Quarterly* 87:533–555.

Calamandrei, S. (2022) Where the Id Was, the Shared Ego Must Now Be: The Acquisition of Symbolic Function, Language and Conscious. *International Journal of Psychoanalysis* 103:761–785.

Cassorla, R. M. (2001) Acute Enactment as a 'Resource' in Disclosing a Collusion Between the Analytical Dyad. *International Journal of Psychoanalysis* 82:1155–1170

Cassorla, R. M. (2008) The Analyst's Implicit Alpha-Function, Trauma and Enactment in the Analysis of Borderline Patients. *International Journal of Psychoanalysis* 89:161–180.

Cassorla, R. M. (2018) *The Psychoanalyst, the Theater of Dreams, and the Clinic of Enactment*. New York and London: Routledge.

Civitarese, G. (2014) *The Necessary Dream*. London: Routledge.

Civitarese, G. (2015) Transformations in Hallucinosis and the Receptivity of the Analyst. *International Journal of Psychoanalysis* 96:1091–1116.

Civitarese, G. (2019) On Bion's Concepts of Negative Capability and Faith. *Psychoanalytic Quarterly* 88:751–783.

Civitarese, G. (2021) The Limits of Interpretation: A Reading of Bion's "On Arrogance". *International Journal of Psychoanalysis* 102:236–257.

Civitarese, G. (2022) Tales of Covid-19: Fear of Contagion and Need for Infection. *Psychoanalytic Quarterly* 91:89–118.

Civitarese, G. (2023a) *Psychoanalytic Field Theory: A Contemporary Introduction*. London and New York: Routledge.

Civitarese, G. (2023b) Invisible-Visual Hallucinations in Bion's "Attacks on Linking". *International Journal of Psychoanalysis* 104:197–222.

Civitarese, G. & Berrini, C. (2022a) On Using Bion's Concepts of Point, Line, and Linking in the Analysis of a 6-Year-Old Child. *Psychoanalytic Dialogues* 32:17–35.

Civitarese, G. & Berrini, C. (2022b) The Aesthetic-Rhizomatic Matrix of Thinking: Reply to Caron Harrang. *Psychoanalytic Dialogues* 32:45–53.

Civitarese, G. & Ferro, A. (2022) *Playing and Vitality in Psychoanalysis*. London: Routledge.

De Masi, F. (2006) Psychotic Withdrawal and the Overthrow of Psychic Reality. *International Journal of Psychoanalysis* 87:789–807.

De Masi, F. (2015) Delusion and Bi-Ocular Vision. *International Journal of Psychoanalysis* 96:1189–1211.

Delourmel, C. (2013) An Introduction to the Work of André Green. *International Journal of Psychoanalysis* 94:133–156.

Ehrlich, R. (2017) Bion's Agony in the Long Week-End. *Journal of the American Psychoanalytic Association* 65:639–664.

Ferro, A. (2002) *In the Analyst's Consulting Room*. East Sussex: Brunner-Routledge.

Ferro, A. (2005) *Seeds of Illness, Seeds of Recovery*. London and New York: Routledge.

Freud, S. (1915) Observations on Transference-Love (Further Recommendations on the Technique of Psycho-Analysis III). *The Standard Edition of the Complete Psychological Works of Sigmund Freud* 12:157–171.

Freud, S. (1917) Mourning and Melancholia. *The Standard Edition of the Complete Psychological Works of Sigmund Freud* 14:237–258.

Freud, S. (1920) Beyond the Pleasure Principle. *The Standard Edition of the Complete Psychological Works of Sigmund Freud* 18:1–64.

Freud, S. (1923) The Ego and the Id. *The Standard Edition of the Complete Psychological Works of Sigmund Freud* 19:1–66.

Green, A. (1986) *On Private Madness*. London: Hogarth Press & The Institute of Psychoanalysis.

Green, A. (1993) *Le travail du negatif*. Paris: Editions de Minuit.[*The Work of the Negative*. London: Free Association Books, 2002]

Green, A. (1999a) On Discriminating and Not Discriminating Between Affect and Representation. *International Journal of Psychoanalysis* 80:277–316.

Green, A. (1999b) *The Work of the Negative*. London: Free Association Books.

Green, A. (2001) *Life Narcissism, Death Narcissism*. London and New York: Free Association Books.

Green, A. (2005) *Key Ideas for a Contemporary Psychoanalysis: Misrecognition and Recognition of the Unconscious*. London and New York: Routledge.

Grotstein, J. S. (1998) BION, W. R. War Memoirs 1917–1919 Francesca Bion (ed.) London: Karnac Books, 1997. Pp. vii + 312. Hbk. £32.50; Pbk. £24.95. *Journal of Analytical Psychology* 43:610–614.

Grotstein, J. S. (2007) *A Beam of Intense Darkness. Wilfred Bion's Legacy to Psychoanalysis*. London: Karnac.

Heidegger, M. (1954) *What Is Called Thinking?* Translated by J. Gray. New York: Harper & Row. 1968.

IPA Inter-Regional Encyclopedic Dictionary of Psychoanalysis. Downloaded February 20, 2023. http://www.ipa.world/ipa/en/Encyclopedic_Dictionary/English/Home.aspx.

Klein, M. (1946) Notes on Some Schizoid Mechanisms. *International Journal of Psychoanalysis* 27:99–110.

Kogan, I. (2015) From Psychic Holes to Psychic Representations. *International Forum of Psychoanalysis* 24:63–76.

Kohon, G. (1999) *The Dead Mother: The Work of André Green*. Edited by G. Kohon. London: Routledge.

Laplanche, J. (1999) *The Unconscious and the Id*. London: Rebus Press.

Laplanche, J. & Pontalis, J. B. (1973) *The Language of Psycho-Analysis*. Translated by D. Nicholson-Smith. London and New York: W. W. Norton & Co.

Levine, H. (2013) The Colorless Canvas. In *Unrepresented States and the Construction of Meaning. Clinical and Theoretical Contributions*, edited by H. Levine, G. Reed & D. Scarfone. London: Karnac, pp. 42–71.

Levine, H. (2021) Trauma, Process and Representation. *International Journal of Psychoanalysis* 102:794–807.

Levine, H. (2022) *Affect, Representation and Language: Between the Silence and the Cry.* London and New York: Routledge.

Levine, H. (2023) Making the Unthinkable Thinkable: Vitalization, Reclamation, Containment, and Representation. In *Autistic Phenomena and Unrepresented States. Explorations in the Emergence of the Self*, edited by H. Levine & J. Santamaría. Oxfordshire: Pheonix.

Levine, H., Reed, G. & Scarfone, D. (2013) *Unrepresented States and the Construction of Meaning: Clinical and Theoretical Contributions*. London: Karnac.

Lewin, B. D. (1946) Sleep, the Mouth, and the Dream Screen. *The Psychoanalytic Quarterly* 15:419–434.

Likierman, M. (2012) "If I Knew Where the Enemy, or Even Germany Was, We Could Have Fired in that Direction": Bion's Experience of War. *Journal of Child Psychotherapy* 38:352–363.

Lopez-Corvo, R. (2003) *The Dictionary of the Work of W. R. Bion*. London: Karnac.

Malin, B. (2021) R. B. Braithwaite's Influence on Bion's Epistemological Contributions. *International Journal of Psychoanalysis* 102:653–670.

Mawson, C. (2014) Editors Introduction. In *Complete Works*, XII, edited by C. Mawson. London: Routledge.

Mawson, C. (2019) *Psychoanalysis and Anxiety: From Knowing to Being*. London: Routledge.

Meltzer, D. (1975) *Explorations in Autism*. London: Harris Meltzer Trust. 2018.

Meltzer, D. (1978) *The Kleinian Development*, Vol. 3. London: Harris Meltzer Trust. 2018.

Meltzer, D. (1986) *Studies in Extended Metapsychology: Clinical Applications of Bion's Ideas*. London: Harris Meltzer Trust. 2018.

Meltzer, D. (1992) *The Claustrum*. London: Harris Meltzer Trust.

Meltzer, D. & Scolmati, A. (2009) Psychotic Illness in Early Childhood: Ten Years on from Explorations in Autism. In *Studies in Extended Metapsychology: Clinical Applications of Bion's Ideas*. London: Karnac.

Meltzer, D. & Williams, M. H. ([1988] 2018) *The Apprehension of Beauty*. London: Harris Meltzer Trust.

Mijola, A. (2002–2005) *International Dictionary of Psychoanalysis*. New York and London: Macmillan, US Thompson.

Neri, C. (2009) The Enlarged Notion of Field in Psychoanalysis. In *The Analytic Field. A Clinical Concept*, edited by A. Ferro & R. Basile. London: Karnac.

Ogden, T. H. (2003) On not being able to dream. *International Journal of Psychoanalysis* 84:17-30

Ogden, T. H. (2004) The Analytic Third: Implications for Psychoanalytic Theory and Technique. *Psychoanalytic Quarterly* 73:167–195.

Ogden, T. H. (2014) Fear of Breakdown and the Unlived Life. *International Journal of Psychoanalysis* 95:205–223.

Ogden, T. H. (2017) Dreaming the Analytic Session: A Clinical Essay. *Psychoanalytic Quarterly* 86:1–20.

Ogden, T. H. (2022) *Coming to Life in the Consulting Room*. London: Routledge.

Perelberg, R. J. (2015) *Murdered Father, Dead Father. Revisting the Oedipus Complex*. Oxon: Routledge.

Perelberg, R. J. (2017) Introduction: André Green: The Arborescence of a Conceptual Paradigm. In *The Greening of Psychoanalysis: André Green's New Paradigm in Contemporary Theory and Practice*, edited by R. J. Perelberg & G. Kohon. London: Routledge.

Perelberg, R. J. & Kohon, G. (2017) *The Greening of Psychoanalysis: André Green's New Paradigm in Contemporary Theory and Practice*. London: Routledge.

Pichon-Rivière, E. (1956–1957) *Teoría del Vínculo*. Buenos Aires: Ediciones Nueva Visión, p. 126. 2002.

Poem Depicts War Scenes. (November 12, 1968) *Regina Leader-Post*, p. 13. Retrieved February 23, 2023.

Quinodoz, D. (1996) An Adopted Analysand's Transference of a "Hole-Object". *International Journal of Psychoanalysis* 77:323–336.

Reed, G. S. & Baudry, F. D. (2005) Conflict, Structure, and Absence: André Green on Borderline and Narcissistic Pathology. *Psychoanalytic Quarterly* 74:121–155.

Ribeiro, M. (2022) The Psychoanalytical Intuition and Reverie: Capturing Facts Not Yet Dreamed. *International Journal of Psychoanalysis* 103:929–947.

Rice, A. K. (1981) Memorial Meeting for Dr Wilfred Bion. *International Review of Psychoanalysis* 8:3–14.

Rocha Barros, E. D. (2000) Affect and Pictographic Image: The Constitution of Meaning in Mental Life. *International Journal of Psychoanalysis* 81:1087–1099.

Rosenberg, B. (1988) Pulsion de mort, négation et travail psychique ou: La pulsion de mort mise au service de la défense contre la pulsion de mort. In *Pouvoirs du négatif dans la psychanalyse et de la culture*. Paris: Champ-Vallon, Seyssel, pp. 65–73.

Rosenberg, B. (2003) *Masochisme Mortifère, Masochisme Gardien de La Vie*. Paris: PUF Editions.

Rycroft, C. (1995) *A Critical Dictionary of Psychoanalysis*. New York: Penguin Books.

Sandler, P. C. (2005) *The Language of Bion: A Dictionary of Concepts*. London: Karnac.

Sandler, P. C. (2009) *A Clinical Application of Bion's Concepts, Vol. 1: Dreaming, Transformations, Containment and Change*. London: Karnac.

Sandler, P. C. (2015) Commentary on "Transformations in Hallucinosis and the Receptivity of the Analyst" by Civitarese. *International Journal of Psychoanalysis* 96:1139–1157.

Segal, H. (1957) Notes on Symbol Formation. *International Journal of Psychoanalysis* 38:391–397.

Sekoff, J. (2022) "I'm Shaking Like Milk": The Immutable Passions of Hypochondria. *Fort Da* 28:32–39.

Souter, K. M. (2009) The War Memoirs: Some Origins of the Thought of W. R. Bion. *International Journal of Psychoanalysis* 90:795–808.

Sparer, E. A. (2010) The French Model at Work: Indication and the Jean Favreau Centre for Consultation and Treatment. *International Journal of Psychoanalysis* 91:1179–1199.

Steiner, J. (2018) The Trauma and Disillusionment of Oedipus. *International Journal of Psychoanalysis* 99:555–568.

Waddell, M. (2011) "From Resemblance to Identity": The Internal Narrative of A Fifty-Minute Hour. In *Bion Today*, edited by C. Mawson. London: Routledge, pp. 366–380.

Williams, M. H. (2010) *Bion's Dream: A Reading of the Autobiographies*. London: Karnac.

Williams, M. H. (2022) *Donald Meltzer. A Contemporary Introduction*. London: Routledge.

Wilson, M. (2020) *The Analyst's Desire: The Ethical Foundations of Clinical Practice*. New York: Bloomsbury Academic.

Winnicott, D. W. (1974) Fear of Breakdown. *International Review of Psychoanalysis* 1:103–107.

Index

Note: Page numbers followed by 'n' and a number indicate a note.

For Product Safety Concerns and Information please contact our EU
representative GPSR@taylorandfrancis.com
Taylor & Francis Verlag GmbH, Kaufingerstraße 24, 80331 München, Germany

www.ingramcontent.com/pod-product-compliance
Lightning Source LLC
Chambersburg PA
CBHW050614280326
41932CB00016B/3033